MORE Minute Math Drills
ADDITION & SUBTRACTION

Carson-Dellosa Publishing Company, Inc.
Greensboro, North Carolina

Credits

Editor: Barrie Hoople

Layout Design: Lori Jackson and Julie Kinlaw

Cover Design: Lori Jackson

Cover Illustration: Ray Lambert

ISBN: 978-1-60418-035-0

03-028131151

Table of Contents

How to Use This Book

More Minute Math Drills: Addition and Subtraction is designed to help students build math fluency in just minutes each day. Each student's objective is to complete one drill page with 100% accuracy within a given time period.

This teacher-friendly book features four types of worksheets to help students who learn at different rates. There are drill pages with 25 problems to introduce students to each section. Drill pages with 50 and 60 problems are divided with cut lines after 10 or 12 problems. Each of these pages can be used as one drill page or cut apart for students who need to focus on a small number of problems. Students should not be timed when the page is cut apart. Activity worksheets reinforce the skills being taught in an easy-to-understand and entertaining format.

Make a copy of the Addition and Subtraction Table on page 5 for each student to reference before completing drill pages.

Use the following suggested time limits for students to complete one drill page. Each suggested time limit may be adjusted to meet students' needs.

First grade: 3–5 minutes
Second grade: 2–4 minutes
Third grade: 1–3 minutes

Before beginning, tell students the amount of time they have to complete the worksheet. Have each student mark the time at the top of her drill page as shown. Note: These minute bubbles only appear on drill pages.

Tell students when to begin and when to stop. Then, have students exchange papers and mark any incorrect answers as you read the answers aloud. Do not give credit for incomplete answers. An answer key is provided on pages 122–128 to assist with assessment. Write each student's grade as a percentage or a fraction in the score bubble at the top of her drill page. Round scores if necessary.

Grades may be recorded on the Score Sheet on page 6. Make a copy for each student and ask her to keep track of her scores. This sheet will motivate students to beat their previous scores.

You may award students with certificates after they master each skill. Award certificates are provided on pages 7 and 8.

Addition and Subtraction Table

+/−	0	1	2	3	4	5	6	7	8	9
0	0	1	2	3	4	5	6	7	8	9
1	1	2	3	4	5	6	7	8	9	10
2	2	3	4	5	6	7	8	9	10	11
3	3	4	5	6	7	8	9	10	11	12
4	4	5	6	7	8	9	10	11	12	13
5	5	6	7	8	9	10	11	12	13	14
6	6	7	8	9	10	11	12	13	14	15
7	7	8	9	10	11	12	13	14	15	16
8	8	9	10	11	12	13	14	15	16	17
9	9	10	11	12	13	14	15	16	17	18

To use the Addition and Subtraction Table to add, pick two numbers to add. Find the first addend in the left column. Slide your finger across that row until you are in the column of the second addend. The number in this box is the sum. For example, if you are adding 6 + 3, start at 6 in the left column. Slide your finger across until it is even with 3 in the top column. Nine is the sum.

To use the Addition and Subtraction Table to subtract, pick two numbers to subtract. Find the subtrahend in the left column. Slide your finger across the row to the minuend. Then, slide your finger up from the minuend to the top row. The number in this box is the difference. For example, if you are subtracting 12 − 8, find 8 in the left column and slide your finger across to 12. Then, slide your finger up from 12 to the top row. Four is the difference.

SCORE SHEET

Name _____

Page	Time	0–69	70	71	72	73	74	75	76	77	78	79	80	81	82	83	84	85	86	87	88	89	90	91	92	93	94	95	96	97	98	99	100

Certificate
of
ACHIEVEMENT

Name

This certificate is presented
for attaining 100% accuracy
within a _____ minute time limit
on More Minute Math drills!

Certificate
of
ACHIEVEMENT

Name

This certificate is presented
for attaining 100% accuracy
within a _____ minute time limit
on More Minute Math drills!

Fast Facts Award

_____

has demonstrated the ability
to think quickly and accurately
when working _____ problems.

Signature: _____

Date: _____

Fast Facts Award

_____

has demonstrated the ability
to think quickly and accurately
when working _____ problems.

Signature: _____

Date: _____

Score

Adding 3

1 2 3 4 5
Minutes

A. 3
   + 3

B. 8
   + 3

C. 3
   + 5

D. 3
   + 0

E. 4
   + 3

F. 3
   + 1

G. 6
   + 3

H. 3
   + 7

I. 3
   + 2

J. 9
   + 3

K. 3
   + 5

L. 4
   + 3

M. 3
   + 8

N. 3
   + 3

O. 3
   + 6

P. 2
   + 3

Q. 3
   + 7

R. 3
   + 9

S. 0
   + 3

T. 1
   + 3

U. 3
   + 2

V. 5
   + 3

W. 3
   + 3

X. 3
   + 6

Y. 8
   + 3

Adding 3

Solve each problem. Help the frog find her friend.

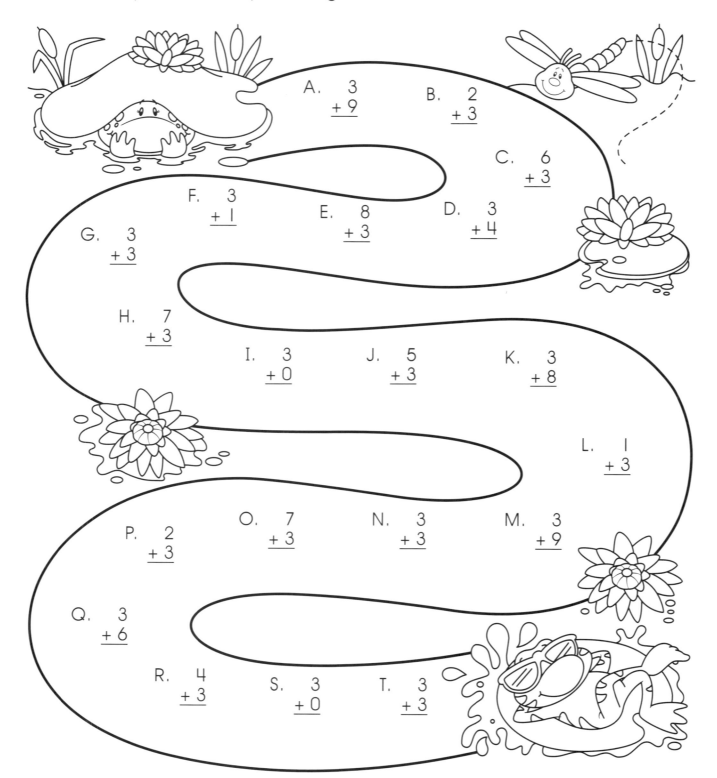

A. $\begin{array}{r} 3 \\ +\,9 \\ \hline \end{array}$

B. $\begin{array}{r} 2 \\ +\,3 \\ \hline \end{array}$

C. $\begin{array}{r} 6 \\ +\,3 \\ \hline \end{array}$

F. $\begin{array}{r} 3 \\ +\,1 \\ \hline \end{array}$

E. $\begin{array}{r} 8 \\ +\,3 \\ \hline \end{array}$

D. $\begin{array}{r} 3 \\ +\,4 \\ \hline \end{array}$

G. $\begin{array}{r} 3 \\ +\,3 \\ \hline \end{array}$

H. $\begin{array}{r} 7 \\ +\,3 \\ \hline \end{array}$

I. $\begin{array}{r} 3 \\ +\,0 \\ \hline \end{array}$

J. $\begin{array}{r} 5 \\ +\,3 \\ \hline \end{array}$

K. $\begin{array}{r} 3 \\ +\,8 \\ \hline \end{array}$

L. $\begin{array}{r} 1 \\ +\,3 \\ \hline \end{array}$

P. $\begin{array}{r} 2 \\ +\,3 \\ \hline \end{array}$

O. $\begin{array}{r} 7 \\ +\,3 \\ \hline \end{array}$

N. $\begin{array}{r} 3 \\ +\,3 \\ \hline \end{array}$

M. $\begin{array}{r} 3 \\ +\,9 \\ \hline \end{array}$

Q. $\begin{array}{r} 3 \\ +\,6 \\ \hline \end{array}$

R. $\begin{array}{r} 4 \\ +\,3 \\ \hline \end{array}$

S. $\begin{array}{r} 3 \\ +\,0 \\ \hline \end{array}$

T. $\begin{array}{r} 3 \\ +\,3 \\ \hline \end{array}$

Name: _____   Date: _____

Adding 3

Solve each problem. Then, color the picture.

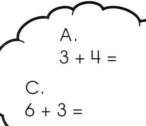

A.
3 + 4 =

C.
6 + 3 =

B.
3 + 3 =

D.   9
   + 3

E.   3
   + 7

I.   8
   + 3

F.
1 + 3 =

G.
0 + 3 =

H.
5 + 3 =

J.
2 + 3 =

K.
3 + 5 =

L.
3 + 9 =

M.
2 + 3 =

N.   3
   + 3

P.
8 + 3 =

O.
6 + 3 =

Q.
4 + 3 =

U.
3 + 4 =

R.   3
   + 0

S.   7
   + 3

T.
1 + 3 =

V.   1
   + 3

W.
3 + 8 =

X.
2 + 3 =

Y.   6
   + 3

1 2 3 4 5
Minutes

Adding 3

Score

A.
$$\begin{array}{r} 3 \\ + 6 \\ \hline \end{array}$$
$$\begin{array}{r} 3 \\ + 2 \\ \hline \end{array}$$
$$\begin{array}{r} 0 \\ + 3 \\ \hline \end{array}$$
$$\begin{array}{r} 3 \\ + 4 \\ \hline \end{array}$$
$$\begin{array}{r} 1 \\ + 3 \\ \hline \end{array}$$

B.
$$\begin{array}{r} 3 \\ + 3 \\ \hline \end{array}$$
$$\begin{array}{r} 3 \\ + 5 \\ \hline \end{array}$$
$$\begin{array}{r} 9 \\ + 3 \\ \hline \end{array}$$
$$\begin{array}{r} 7 \\ + 3 \\ \hline \end{array}$$
$$\begin{array}{r} 3 \\ + 8 \\ \hline \end{array}$$

C.
$$\begin{array}{r} 8 \\ + 3 \\ \hline \end{array}$$
$$\begin{array}{r} 4 \\ + 3 \\ \hline \end{array}$$
$$\begin{array}{r} 2 \\ + 3 \\ \hline \end{array}$$
$$\begin{array}{r} 6 \\ + 3 \\ \hline \end{array}$$
$$\begin{array}{r} 1 \\ + 3 \\ \hline \end{array}$$

D.
$$\begin{array}{r} 5 \\ + 3 \\ \hline \end{array}$$
$$\begin{array}{r} 3 \\ + 3 \\ \hline \end{array}$$
$$\begin{array}{r} 0 \\ + 3 \\ \hline \end{array}$$
$$\begin{array}{r} 9 \\ + 3 \\ \hline \end{array}$$
$$\begin{array}{r} 7 \\ + 3 \\ \hline \end{array}$$

E.
$$\begin{array}{r} 2 \\ + 3 \\ \hline \end{array}$$
$$\begin{array}{r} 3 \\ + 5 \\ \hline \end{array}$$
$$\begin{array}{r} 3 \\ + 3 \\ \hline \end{array}$$
$$\begin{array}{r} 6 \\ + 3 \\ \hline \end{array}$$
$$\begin{array}{r} 8 \\ + 3 \\ \hline \end{array}$$

F.
$$\begin{array}{r} 7 \\ + 3 \\ \hline \end{array}$$
$$\begin{array}{r} 3 \\ + 4 \\ \hline \end{array}$$
$$\begin{array}{r} 0 \\ + 3 \\ \hline \end{array}$$
$$\begin{array}{r} 1 \\ + 3 \\ \hline \end{array}$$
$$\begin{array}{r} 3 \\ + 9 \\ \hline \end{array}$$

G.
$$\begin{array}{r} 1 \\ + 3 \\ \hline \end{array}$$
$$\begin{array}{r} 9 \\ + 3 \\ \hline \end{array}$$
$$\begin{array}{r} 3 \\ + 5 \\ \hline \end{array}$$
$$\begin{array}{r} 3 \\ + 3 \\ \hline \end{array}$$
$$\begin{array}{r} 3 \\ + 8 \\ \hline \end{array}$$

H.
$$\begin{array}{r} 2 \\ + 3 \\ \hline \end{array}$$
$$\begin{array}{r} 3 \\ + 6 \\ \hline \end{array}$$
$$\begin{array}{r} 1 \\ + 3 \\ \hline \end{array}$$
$$\begin{array}{r} 3 \\ + 7 \\ \hline \end{array}$$
$$\begin{array}{r} 4 \\ + 3 \\ \hline \end{array}$$

I.
$$\begin{array}{r} 3 \\ + 9 \\ \hline \end{array}$$
$$\begin{array}{r} 0 \\ + 3 \\ \hline \end{array}$$
$$\begin{array}{r} 3 \\ + 5 \\ \hline \end{array}$$
$$\begin{array}{r} 8 \\ + 3 \\ \hline \end{array}$$
$$\begin{array}{r} 3 \\ + 4 \\ \hline \end{array}$$

J.
$$\begin{array}{r} 6 \\ + 3 \\ \hline \end{array}$$
$$\begin{array}{r} 1 \\ + 3 \\ \hline \end{array}$$
$$\begin{array}{r} 7 \\ + 3 \\ \hline \end{array}$$
$$\begin{array}{r} 0 \\ + 3 \\ \hline \end{array}$$
$$\begin{array}{r} 3 \\ + 2 \\ \hline \end{array}$$

Name: _____ Date: _____

A.
$$\begin{array}{r}1\\+0\\\hline\end{array}\qquad\begin{array}{r}5\\+1\\\hline\end{array}\qquad\begin{array}{r}0\\+2\\\hline\end{array}\qquad\begin{array}{r}1\\+3\\\hline\end{array}\qquad\begin{array}{r}3\\+2\\\hline\end{array}\qquad\begin{array}{r}9\\+2\\\hline\end{array}$$

B.
$$\begin{array}{r}1\\+6\\\hline\end{array}\qquad\begin{array}{r}4\\+1\\\hline\end{array}\qquad\begin{array}{r}5\\+3\\\hline\end{array}\qquad\begin{array}{r}1\\+9\\\hline\end{array}\qquad\begin{array}{r}8\\+3\\\hline\end{array}\qquad\begin{array}{r}6\\+2\\\hline\end{array}$$

C.
$$\begin{array}{r}2\\+9\\\hline\end{array}\qquad\begin{array}{r}5\\+1\\\hline\end{array}\qquad\begin{array}{r}1\\+1\\\hline\end{array}\qquad\begin{array}{r}2\\+5\\\hline\end{array}\qquad\begin{array}{r}4\\+1\\\hline\end{array}\qquad\begin{array}{r}5\\+3\\\hline\end{array}$$

D.
$$\begin{array}{r}8\\+1\\\hline\end{array}\qquad\begin{array}{r}2\\+7\\\hline\end{array}\qquad\begin{array}{r}2\\+1\\\hline\end{array}\qquad\begin{array}{r}9\\+3\\\hline\end{array}\qquad\begin{array}{r}1\\+0\\\hline\end{array}\qquad\begin{array}{r}6\\+1\\\hline\end{array}$$

E.
$$\begin{array}{r}7\\+3\\\hline\end{array}\qquad\begin{array}{r}1\\+5\\\hline\end{array}\qquad\begin{array}{r}0\\+3\\\hline\end{array}\qquad\begin{array}{r}8\\+3\\\hline\end{array}\qquad\begin{array}{r}9\\+2\\\hline\end{array}\qquad\begin{array}{r}6\\+1\\\hline\end{array}$$

F.
$$\begin{array}{r}3\\+3\\\hline\end{array}\qquad\begin{array}{r}5\\+2\\\hline\end{array}\qquad\begin{array}{r}1\\+4\\\hline\end{array}\qquad\begin{array}{r}3\\+6\\\hline\end{array}\qquad\begin{array}{r}2\\+2\\\hline\end{array}\qquad\begin{array}{r}3\\+5\\\hline\end{array}$$

G.
$$\begin{array}{r}9\\+2\\\hline\end{array}\qquad\begin{array}{r}3\\+4\\\hline\end{array}\qquad\begin{array}{r}2\\+1\\\hline\end{array}\qquad\begin{array}{r}1\\+9\\\hline\end{array}\qquad\begin{array}{r}8\\+2\\\hline\end{array}\qquad\begin{array}{r}6\\+2\\\hline\end{array}$$

H.
$$\begin{array}{r}3\\+1\\\hline\end{array}\qquad\begin{array}{r}0\\+2\\\hline\end{array}\qquad\begin{array}{r}5\\+1\\\hline\end{array}\qquad\begin{array}{r}2\\+1\\\hline\end{array}\qquad\begin{array}{r}4\\+3\\\hline\end{array}\qquad\begin{array}{r}6\\+3\\\hline\end{array}$$

I.
$$\begin{array}{r}2\\+5\\\hline\end{array}\qquad\begin{array}{r}0\\+3\\\hline\end{array}\qquad\begin{array}{r}1\\+9\\\hline\end{array}\qquad\begin{array}{r}2\\+2\\\hline\end{array}\qquad\begin{array}{r}3\\+0\\\hline\end{array}\qquad\begin{array}{r}3\\+1\\\hline\end{array}$$

J.
$$\begin{array}{r}2\\+4\\\hline\end{array}\qquad\begin{array}{r}1\\+8\\\hline\end{array}\qquad\begin{array}{r}2\\+3\\\hline\end{array}\qquad\begin{array}{r}3\\+4\\\hline\end{array}\qquad\begin{array}{r}9\\+2\\\hline\end{array}\qquad\begin{array}{r}1\\+1\\\hline\end{array}$$

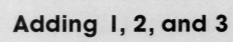

Adding 1, 2, and 3

Solve each problem. Circle each problem and answer in the puzzle. Problems can be hidden across or down. The first one has been done for you.

A. 5 + 1 = **6**   1 + 2 =   2 + 3 =   4 + 3 =   5 + 3 =

B. 3 + 1 =   6 + 3 =   4 + 2 =   7 + 2 =   5 + 2 =

Name: _____ Date: _____

Adding 1, 2, and 3

Solve each problem. Then, use the color key to color the picture.

Color Key

5 = red   **6 = brown**   **7 = yellow**

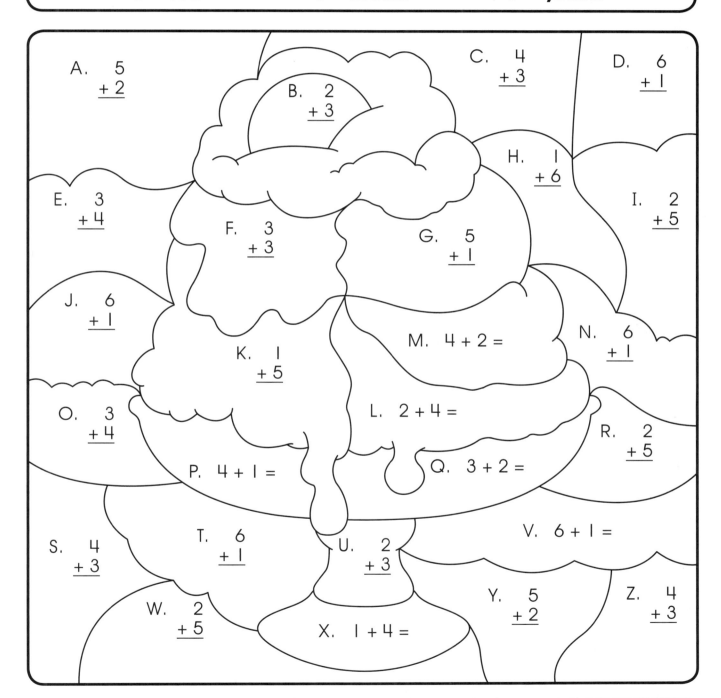

A.   5
    + 2

B.   2
    + 3

C.   4
    + 3

D.   6
    + 1

E.   3
    + 4

F.   3
    + 3

G.   5
    + 1

H.   1
    + 6

I.   2
    + 5

J.   6
    + 1

K.   1
    + 5

L.   2 + 4 =

M.   4 + 2 =

N.   6
    + 1

O.   3
    + 4

P.   4 + 1 =

Q.   3 + 2 =

R.   2
    + 5

S.   4
    + 3

T.   6
    + 1

U.   2
    + 3

V.   6 + 1 =

W.   2
    + 5

X.   1 + 4 =

Y.   5
    + 2

Z.   4
    + 3

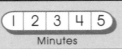 Name: _____ Date: _____

| 1 | 2 | 3 | 4 | 5 |
Minutes

Adding 1, 2, and 3

 Score

A.
$\begin{array}{r} 1 \\ + 3 \\ \hline \end{array}$
$\begin{array}{r} 2 \\ + 5 \\ \hline \end{array}$
$\begin{array}{r} 0 \\ + 1 \\ \hline \end{array}$
$\begin{array}{r} 1 \\ + 8 \\ \hline \end{array}$
$\begin{array}{r} 7 \\ + 2 \\ \hline \end{array}$
$\begin{array}{r} 6 \\ + 2 \\ \hline \end{array}$

B.
$\begin{array}{r} 1 \\ + 0 \\ \hline \end{array}$
$\begin{array}{r} 6 \\ + 3 \\ \hline \end{array}$
$\begin{array}{r} 3 \\ + 7 \\ \hline \end{array}$
$\begin{array}{r} 9 \\ + 3 \\ \hline \end{array}$
$\begin{array}{r} 3 \\ + 4 \\ \hline \end{array}$
$\begin{array}{r} 8 \\ + 2 \\ \hline \end{array}$

C.
$\begin{array}{r} 5 \\ + 1 \\ \hline \end{array}$
$\begin{array}{r} 3 \\ + 8 \\ \hline \end{array}$
$\begin{array}{r} 6 \\ + 1 \\ \hline \end{array}$
$\begin{array}{r} 9 \\ + 2 \\ \hline \end{array}$
$\begin{array}{r} 1 \\ + 4 \\ \hline \end{array}$
$\begin{array}{r} 3 \\ + 5 \\ \hline \end{array}$

D.
$\begin{array}{r} 2 \\ + 2 \\ \hline \end{array}$
$\begin{array}{r} 2 \\ + 0 \\ \hline \end{array}$
$\begin{array}{r} 4 \\ + 3 \\ \hline \end{array}$
$\begin{array}{r} 2 \\ + 7 \\ \hline \end{array}$
$\begin{array}{r} 0 \\ + 1 \\ \hline \end{array}$
$\begin{array}{r} 3 \\ + 3 \\ \hline \end{array}$

E.
$\begin{array}{r} 2 \\ + 9 \\ \hline \end{array}$
$\begin{array}{r} 8 \\ + 1 \\ \hline \end{array}$
$\begin{array}{r} 6 \\ + 3 \\ \hline \end{array}$
$\begin{array}{r} 2 \\ + 4 \\ \hline \end{array}$
$\begin{array}{r} 2 \\ + 8 \\ \hline \end{array}$
$\begin{array}{r} 6 \\ + 1 \\ \hline \end{array}$

F.
$\begin{array}{r} 1 \\ + 1 \\ \hline \end{array}$
$\begin{array}{r} 7 \\ + 2 \\ \hline \end{array}$
$\begin{array}{r} 3 \\ + 9 \\ \hline \end{array}$
$\begin{array}{r} 2 \\ + 1 \\ \hline \end{array}$
$\begin{array}{r} 4 \\ + 2 \\ \hline \end{array}$
$\begin{array}{r} 3 \\ + 7 \\ \hline \end{array}$

G.
$\begin{array}{r} 5 \\ + 1 \\ \hline \end{array}$
$\begin{array}{r} 3 \\ + 3 \\ \hline \end{array}$
$\begin{array}{r} 0 \\ + 1 \\ \hline \end{array}$
$\begin{array}{r} 0 \\ + 2 \\ \hline \end{array}$
$\begin{array}{r} 6 \\ + 3 \\ \hline \end{array}$
$\begin{array}{r} 7 \\ + 1 \\ \hline \end{array}$

H.
$\begin{array}{r} 3 \\ + 8 \\ \hline \end{array}$
$\begin{array}{r} 9 \\ + 1 \\ \hline \end{array}$
$\begin{array}{r} 2 \\ + 5 \\ \hline \end{array}$
$\begin{array}{r} 8 \\ + 1 \\ \hline \end{array}$
$\begin{array}{r} 4 \\ + 2 \\ \hline \end{array}$
$\begin{array}{r} 1 \\ + 9 \\ \hline \end{array}$

I.
$\begin{array}{r} 1 \\ + 2 \\ \hline \end{array}$
$\begin{array}{r} 3 \\ + 0 \\ \hline \end{array}$
$\begin{array}{r} 9 \\ + 1 \\ \hline \end{array}$
$\begin{array}{r} 5 \\ + 1 \\ \hline \end{array}$
$\begin{array}{r} 1 \\ + 3 \\ \hline \end{array}$
$\begin{array}{r} 3 \\ + 2 \\ \hline \end{array}$

J.
$\begin{array}{r} 2 \\ + 2 \\ \hline \end{array}$
$\begin{array}{r} 1 \\ + 6 \\ \hline \end{array}$
$\begin{array}{r} 8 \\ + 3 \\ \hline \end{array}$
$\begin{array}{r} 4 \\ + 1 \\ \hline \end{array}$
$\begin{array}{r} 7 \\ + 3 \\ \hline \end{array}$
$\begin{array}{r} 3 \\ + 4 \\ \hline \end{array}$

Adding 4

A. $\begin{array}{r} 4 \\ +1 \\ \hline \end{array}$ B. $\begin{array}{r} 2 \\ +4 \\ \hline \end{array}$ C. $\begin{array}{r} 5 \\ +4 \\ \hline \end{array}$ D. $\begin{array}{r} 4 \\ +3 \\ \hline \end{array}$ E. $\begin{array}{r} 8 \\ +4 \\ \hline \end{array}$

F. $\begin{array}{r} 4 \\ +0 \\ \hline \end{array}$ G. $\begin{array}{r} 4 \\ +6 \\ \hline \end{array}$ H. $\begin{array}{r} 1 \\ +4 \\ \hline \end{array}$ I. $\begin{array}{r} 4 \\ +7 \\ \hline \end{array}$ J. $\begin{array}{r} 2 \\ +4 \\ \hline \end{array}$

K. $\begin{array}{r} 4 \\ +9 \\ \hline \end{array}$ L. $\begin{array}{r} 4 \\ +3 \\ \hline \end{array}$ M. $\begin{array}{r} 6 \\ +4 \\ \hline \end{array}$ N. $\begin{array}{r} 4 \\ +1 \\ \hline \end{array}$ O. $\begin{array}{r} 0 \\ +4 \\ \hline \end{array}$

P. $\begin{array}{r} 5 \\ +4 \\ \hline \end{array}$ Q. $\begin{array}{r} 4 \\ +7 \\ \hline \end{array}$ R. $\begin{array}{r} 4 \\ +4 \\ \hline \end{array}$ S. $\begin{array}{r} 4 \\ +8 \\ \hline \end{array}$ T. $\begin{array}{r} 9 \\ +4 \\ \hline \end{array}$

U. $\begin{array}{r} 4 \\ +6 \\ \hline \end{array}$ V. $\begin{array}{r} 5 \\ +4 \\ \hline \end{array}$ W. $\begin{array}{r} 2 \\ +4 \\ \hline \end{array}$ X. $\begin{array}{r} 4 \\ +0 \\ \hline \end{array}$ Y. $\begin{array}{r} 3 \\ +4 \\ \hline \end{array}$

Name: _____ Date: _____

Adding 4

Solve each problem.

A.
$$\begin{array}{r} 4 \\ +2 \\ \hline \end{array}$$
$$\begin{array}{r} 4 \\ +4 \\ \hline \end{array}$$
$$\begin{array}{r} 4 \\ +3 \\ \hline \end{array}$$
$$\begin{array}{r} 1 \\ +4 \\ \hline \end{array}$$
$$\begin{array}{r} 0 \\ +4 \\ \hline \end{array}$$

B.
$$\begin{array}{r} 8 \\ +4 \\ \hline \end{array}$$
$$\begin{array}{r} 9 \\ +4 \\ \hline \end{array}$$
$$\begin{array}{r} 4 \\ +3 \\ \hline \end{array}$$
$$\begin{array}{r} 6 \\ +4 \\ \hline \end{array}$$

C.
$$\begin{array}{r} 7 \\ +4 \\ \hline \end{array}$$
$$\begin{array}{r} 9 \\ +4 \\ \hline \end{array}$$
$$\begin{array}{r} 4 \\ +0 \\ \hline \end{array}$$

D.
$$\begin{array}{r} 4 \\ +1 \\ \hline \end{array}$$
$$\begin{array}{r} 2 \\ +4 \\ \hline \end{array}$$
$$\begin{array}{r} 4 \\ +7 \\ \hline \end{array}$$
$$\begin{array}{r} 4 \\ +4 \\ \hline \end{array}$$
$$\begin{array}{r} 4 \\ +3 \\ \hline \end{array}$$

E.
$$\begin{array}{r} 6 \\ +4 \\ \hline \end{array}$$
$$\begin{array}{r} 9 \\ +4 \\ \hline \end{array}$$
$$\begin{array}{r} 4 \\ +1 \\ \hline \end{array}$$

F.
$$\begin{array}{r} 4 \\ +4 \\ \hline \end{array}$$
$$\begin{array}{r} 4 \\ +2 \\ \hline \end{array}$$
$$\begin{array}{r} 4 \\ +7 \\ \hline \end{array}$$
$$\begin{array}{r} 6 \\ +4 \\ \hline \end{array}$$
$$\begin{array}{r} 3 \\ +4 \\ \hline \end{array}$$

Adding 4

Solve each problem. Help the duckling find his family.

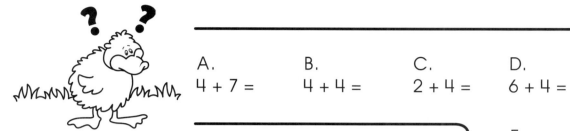

A.	B.	C.	D.
4 + 7 =	4 + 4 =	2 + 4 =	6 + 4 =

E.
4 + 1 =

J.	I.	H.	G.	F.
7 + 4 =	9 + 4 =	4 + 0 =	4 + 3 =	5 + 4 =

K.
4 + 8 =

L.
5 + 4 =

M.	N.	O.	P.	Q.
3 + 4 =	4 + 6 =	2 + 4 =	4 + 7 =	0 + 4 =

R.
4 + 4 =

S.
1 + 4 =

T.
4 + 9 =

A.
```
  4        3        0        5        4
+ 1      + 4      + 4      + 4      + 8
```

B.
```
  1        4        4        0        4
+ 4      + 2      + 7      + 4      + 4
```

C.
```
  4        9        4        4        5
+ 6      + 4      + 3      + 0      + 4
```

D.
```
  4        7        4        4        1
+ 8      + 4      + 9      + 4      + 4
```

E.
```
  2        6        7        4        3
+ 4      + 4      + 4      + 9      + 4
```

F.
```
  4        8        4        1        0
+ 4      + 4      + 6      + 4      + 4
```

G.
```
  2        4        9        8        4
+ 4      + 7      + 4      + 4      + 0
```

H.
```
  4        4        6        5        4
+ 5      + 4      + 4      + 4      + 3
```

I.
```
  4        7        3        4        2
+ 4      + 4      + 4      + 1      + 4
```

J.
```
  5        4        8        4        0
+ 4      + 1      + 4      + 9      + 4
```

Name: _____ Date: _____

A. 0
   + 5

B. 5
   + 1

C. 2
   + 5

D. 5
   + 8

E. 6
   + 5

F. 5
   + 9

G. 5
   + 5

H. 4
   + 5

I. 3
   + 5

J. 5
   + 0

K. 5
   + 2

L. 0
   + 5

M. 9
   + 5

N. 5
   + 4

O. 7
   + 5

P. 2
   + 5

Q. 1
   + 5

R. 5
   + 5

S. 8
   + 5

T. 6
   + 5

U. 7
   + 5

V. 5
   + 8

W. 4
   + 5

X. 5
   + 7

Y. 1
   + 5

Name: _____ Date: _____

Adding 5

Solve each problem. Then, color the picture.

A. 4
  + 5

B. 5
  + 2

C. 5
  + 6

D. 4
  + 5

E. 9
  + 5

F. 0
  + 5

G. 1
  + 5

H. 5
  + 8

I. 9
  + 5

J. 5
  + 0

K. 4
  + 5

L. 7
  + 5

M. 5
  + 2

N. 3
  + 5

O. 6
  + 5

P. 8
  + 5

Q. 5
  + 0

R. 5
  + 4

S. 7
  + 5

T. 2
  + 5

U. 9
  + 5

V. 5
  + 1

Adding 5

Solve each problem.

A.

$5 + 8 =$ $4 + 5 =$ $5 + 2 =$ $6 + 5 =$ $5 + 5 =$

B.

$5 + 5 =$ $3 + 5 =$ $0 + 5 =$ $5 + 9 =$ $7 + 5 =$

C.

$5 + 2 =$ $5 + 5 =$ $5 + 3 =$

D.

$5 + 6 =$ $8 + 5 =$ $7 + 5 =$

E.

$8 + 5 =$ $3 + 5 =$ $2 + 5 =$

F.

$5 + 4 =$ $5 + 0 =$ $6 + 5 =$

G.

$9 + 5 =$ $5 + 5 =$ $5 + 3 =$

Adding 5

Score

A. 4 + 5 =   5 + 5 =   5 + 0 =   3 + 5 =   5 + 2 =

B. 6 + 5 =   5 + 8 =   4 + 5 =   5 + 7 =   9 + 5 =

C. 3 + 5 =   6 + 5 =   5 + 9 =   0 + 5 =   5 + 5 =

D. 5 + 2 =   5 + 4 =   5 + 5 =   8 + 5 =   5 + 7 =

E. 2 + 5 =   9 + 5 =   5 + 0 =   5 + 5 =   7 + 5 =

F. 5 + 5 =   5 + 3 =   8 + 5 =   5 + 4 =   6 + 5 =

G. 4 + 5 =   5 + 7 =   9 + 5 =   5 + 5 =   5 + 3 =

H. 5 + 2 =   1 + 5 =   5 + 6 =   8 + 5 =   5 + 0 =

I. 6 + 5 =   7 + 5 =   3 + 5 =   0 + 5 =   5 + 5 =

J. 5 + 0 =   4 + 5 =   5 + 9 =   2 + 5 =   5 + 7 =

Score

Adding 6

A. 0
    +6

B. 6
    +4

C. 2
    +6

D. 6
    +6

E. 6
    +1

F. 5
    +6

G. 6
    +3

H. 6
    +8

I. 9
    +6

J. 6
    +7

K. 6
    +6

L. 6
    +5

M. 7
    +6

N. 6
    +3

O. 8
    +6

P. 6
    +2

Q. 4
    +6

R. 6
    +0

S. 1
    +6

T. 6
    +9

U. 6
    +3

V. 6
    +2

W. 8
    +6

X. 6
    +6

Y. 6
    +5

Adding 6

Solve each problem. Help the doll find the toy box.

A.
4 + 6 =

B.
6 + 6 =

C.
6 + 7 =

D.
6 + 1 =

E.
6 + 6 =

F.
6 + 0 =

G.
3 + 6 =

H.
6 + 8 =

I.
5 + 6 =

J.
9 + 6 =

K.
6 + 1 =

L.
6 + 6 =

M.
4 + 6 =

N.
6 + 7 =

O.
8 + 6 =

P.
6 + 4 =

Q.
9 + 6 =

R.
5 + 6 =

S.
0 + 6 =

T.
6 + 3 =

Name: _____ Date: _____

Adding 6

Solve each problem. Then, color the picture.

A. 0
+ 6

B. 7
+ 6

C. 1
+ 6

D. 6
+ 8

E. 6 + 5 =

F. 3
+ 6

G. 6
+ 6

H. 6
+ 3

I. 5
+ 6

J. 9
+ 6

K. 6
+ 4

L. 4
+ 6

M. 6 + 0 =

N. 6 + 6 =

O. 6
+ 7

P. 5 + 6 =

Q. 6 + 6 =

R. 3
+ 6

S. 7
+ 6

T. 9
+ 6

U. 3
+ 6

V. 6 + 8 =

W. 6
+ 1

1 2 3 4 5
Minutes

Adding 6

Score

A.
$$6 + 0$$ $$2 + 6$$ $$4 + 6$$ $$6 + 3$$ $$1 + 6$$

B.
$$6 + 6$$ $$6 + 8$$ $$6 + 5$$ $$7 + 6$$ $$6 + 9$$

C.
$$6 + 5$$ $$6 + 6$$ $$6 + 9$$ $$0 + 6$$ $$1 + 6$$

D.
$$4 + 6$$ $$6 + 2$$ $$6 + 3$$ $$8 + 6$$ $$6 + 7$$

E.
$$6 + 6$$ $$9 + 6$$ $$3 + 6$$ $$6 + 4$$ $$7 + 6$$

F.
$$5 + 6$$ $$6 + 0$$ $$6 + 8$$ $$1 + 6$$ $$6 + 2$$

G.
$$4 + 6$$ $$7 + 6$$ $$2 + 6$$ $$6 + 1$$ $$9 + 6$$

H.
$$6 + 6$$ $$5 + 6$$ $$6 + 9$$ $$6 + 7$$ $$0 + 6$$

I.
$$8 + 6$$ $$9 + 6$$ $$3 + 6$$ $$6 + 1$$ $$6 + 5$$

J.
$$0 + 6$$ $$4 + 6$$ $$6 + 6$$ $$2 + 6$$ $$7 + 6$$

Adding 4, 5, and 6

A.	5 + 0	3 + 5	0 + 4	6 + 5	6 + 4	4 + 9
B.	8 + 6	4 + 6	9 + 5	5 + 5	5 + 2	1 + 5
C.	5 + 4	5 + 6	5 + 8	3 + 4	4 + 5	9 + 6
D.	0 + 5	6 + 5	6 + 7	1 + 5	0 + 6	6 + 8
E.	4 + 1	6 + 5	6 + 2	5 + 2	6 + 5	6 + 6
F.	4 + 7	8 + 6	1 + 4	6 + 4	5 + 4	5 + 0
G.	8 + 4	6 + 4	5 + 6	4 + 0	5 + 5	4 + 5
H.	3 + 6	5 + 4	6 + 3	0 + 5	9 + 5	4 + 4
I.	0 + 6	8 + 5	4 + 5	5 + 3	4 + 6	1 + 4
J.	9 + 4	6 + 1	6 + 5	4 + 4	2 + 5	5 + 9

Adding 4, 5, and 6

Solve each problem. Circle each problem and answer in the puzzle. Problems can be hidden across or down. The first one has been done for you.

A. $2 + 4 = \mathbf{6}$ $5 + 4 =$ $0 + 6 =$ $4 + 4 =$ $1 + 6 =$

B. $8 + 4 =$ $1 + 4 =$ $2 + 6 =$ $1 + 5 =$ $3 + 6 =$

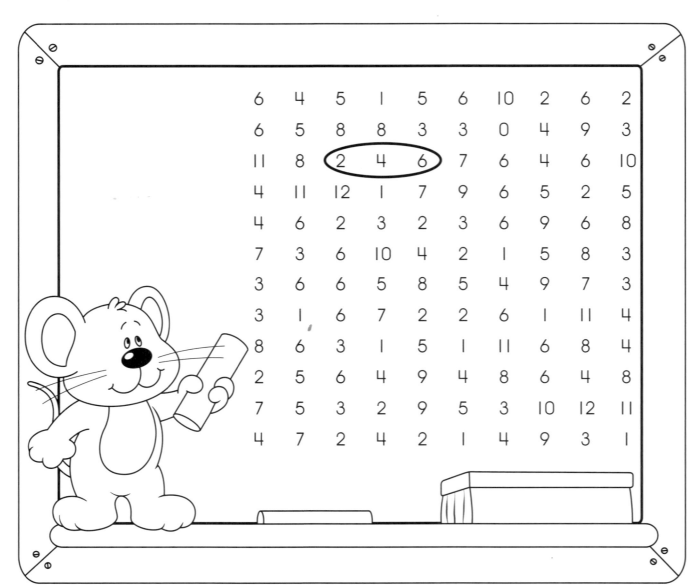

6	4	5	1	5	6	10	2	6	2
6	5	8	8	3	3	0	4	9	3
11	8	2	4	6	7	6	4	6	10
4	11	12	1	7	9	6	5	2	5
4	6	2	3	2	3	6	9	6	8
7	3	6	10	4	2	1	5	8	3
3	6	6	5	8	5	4	9	7	3
3	1	6	7	2	2	6	1	11	4
8	6	3	1	5	1	11	6	8	4
2	5	6	4	9	4	8	6	4	8
7	5	3	2	9	5	3	10	12	11
4	7	2	4	2	1	4	9	3	1

Name: _____ Date: _____

Adding 4, 5, and 6

Solve each problem. Then, use the color key to color the picture.

Color Key

7 = gray	**8 = brown**	**9 = green**

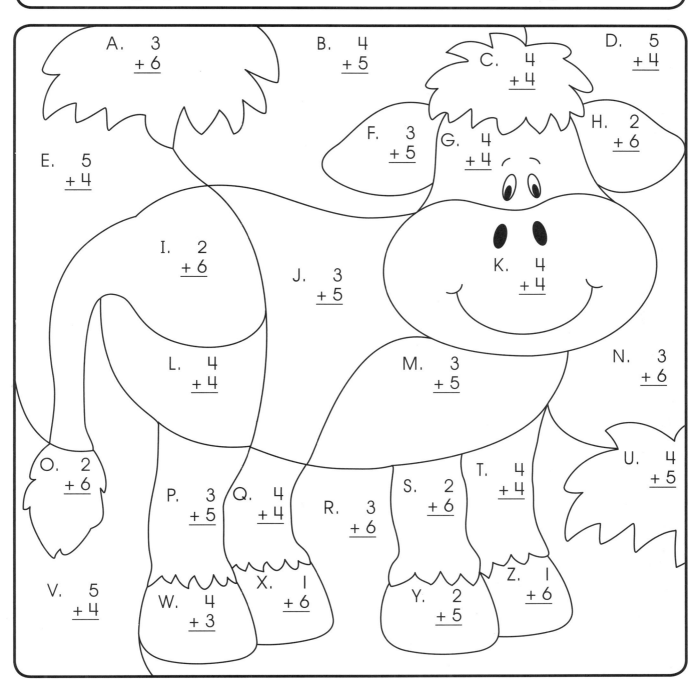

A. 3
  + 6

B. 4
  + 5

C. 4
  + 4

D. 5
  + 4

E. 5
  + 4

F. 3
  + 5

G. 4
  + 4

H. 2
  + 6

I. 2
  + 6

J. 3
  + 5

K. 4
  + 4

L. 4
  + 4

M. 3
  + 5

N. 3
  + 6

O. 2
  + 6

P. 3
  + 5

Q. 4
  + 4

R. 3
  + 6

S. 2
  + 6

T. 4
  + 4

U. 4
  + 5

V. 5
  + 4

W. 4
  + 3

X. 1
  + 6

Y. 2
  + 5

Z. 1
  + 6

A.
$$4 + 3$$
$$2 + 5$$
$$6 + 1$$
$$5 + 1$$
$$2 + 4$$
$$6 + 2$$

B.
$$0 + 5$$
$$6 + 4$$
$$4 + 7$$
$$9 + 6$$
$$3 + 4$$
$$7 + 6$$

C.
$$5 + 4$$
$$4 + 8$$
$$1 + 6$$
$$9 + 4$$
$$4 + 4$$
$$5 + 6$$

D.
$$2 + 6$$
$$5 + 0$$
$$4 + 3$$
$$5 + 2$$
$$0 + 5$$
$$3 + 4$$

E.
$$9 + 5$$
$$6 + 6$$
$$6 + 3$$
$$4 + 4$$
$$4 + 8$$
$$6 + 2$$

F.
$$4 + 1$$
$$4 + 7$$
$$5 + 5$$
$$5 + 3$$
$$4 + 2$$
$$7 + 4$$

G.
$$1 + 5$$
$$4 + 3$$
$$0 + 5$$
$$6 + 4$$
$$5 + 6$$
$$5 + 5$$

H.
$$5 + 3$$
$$6 + 1$$
$$2 + 5$$
$$1 + 6$$
$$2 + 4$$
$$6 + 6$$

I.
$$0 + 6$$
$$6 + 5$$
$$5 + 9$$
$$1 + 5$$
$$4 + 4$$
$$3 + 6$$

J.
$$2 + 4$$
$$6 + 1$$
$$5 + 5$$
$$4 + 3$$
$$3 + 5$$
$$6 + 4$$

Name: _____ Date: _____

Adding 1–6

Solve each problem. Draw a line from each egg to the nest with the matching answer.

A. 6
   + 5

12

B. 0
   + 3

3

C. 7
   + 5

11

D. 0
   + 6

5

E. 1
   + 3

6

F. 4
   + 1

4

G. 2
   + 2

9

H. 3
   + 6

4

I. 5
   + 5

13

J. 9
   + 4

10

K. 1
   + 1

14

L. 9
   + 5

2

A.
0	5	0	4	4	4
+ 1	+ 3	+ 4	+ 4	+ 6	+ 5

B.
6	0	5	9	8	2
+ 5	+ 2	+ 2	+ 3	+ 6	+ 4

C.
9	7	2	5	1	5
+ 1	+ 3	+ 5	+ 5	+ 1	+ 6

D.
8	3	4	9	0	6
+ 5	+ 3	+ 5	+ 6	+ 2	+ 5

E.
1	2	0	8	1	5
+ 3	+ 2	+ 3	+ 6	+ 3	+ 6

F.
0	4	9	3	4	9
+ 2	+ 1	+ 5	+ 3	+ 1	+ 5

G.
1	6	4	0	8	5
+ 3	+ 4	+ 5	+ 5	+ 4	+ 1

H.
6	0	5	8	4	0
+ 5	+ 4	+ 5	+ 5	+ 2	+ 6

I.
2	3	1	4	0	6
+ 4	+ 3	+ 5	+ 2	+ 6	+ 5

J.
4	3	2	4	4	7
+ 5	+ 5	+ 6	+ 1	+ 3	+ 2

Name: _____ Date: _____

Adding 7

1 2 3 4 5
Minutes

A.   7
   + 0

B.   7
   + 4

C.   7
   + 7

D.   6
   + 7

E.   7
   + 1

F.   5
   + 7

G.   7
   + 3

H.   8
   + 7

I.   7
   + 9

J.   7
   + 7

K.   1
   + 7

L.   7
   + 5

M.   7
   + 7

N.   7
   + 3

O.   8
   + 7

P.   7
   + 6

Q.   4
   + 7

R.   0
   + 7

S.   1
   + 7

T.   9
   + 7

U.   3
   + 7

V.   6
   + 7

W.   7
   + 8

X.   7
   + 7

Y.   7
   + 5

Adding 7

Solve each problem.

A.
4 + 7 =
7 + 7 =
7 + 2 =
1 + 7 =
7 + 0 =

B.
6 + 7 =
7 + 3 =
8 + 7 =
7 + 5 =
9 + 7 =

C.
1 + 7 =
7 + 6 =
7 + 7 =
0 + 7 =
4 + 7 =

D.
7 + 9 =
3 + 7 =
5 + 7 =

E.
0 + 7 =
8 + 7 =
7 + 2 =

F.
4 + 7 =
0 + 7 =
7 + 7 =

G.
9 + 7 =
7 + 2 =
4 + 7 =

H.
6 + 7 =
1 + 7 =
7 + 3 =

KIDS
AT
WORK

Score

Adding 7

1 2 3 4 5
Minutes

Solve each problem. Help the monkey find the bananas.

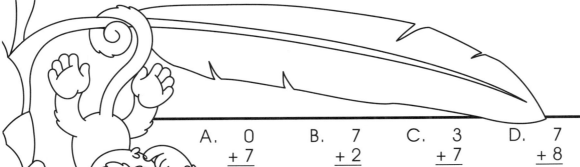

| A. 0
+7 | B. 7
+2 | C. 3
+7 | D. 7
+8 | E. 5
+7 |

| | | | | F. 7
+9 |

| L. 7
+5 | K. 7
+7 | J. 7
+1 | I. 4
+7 | H. 6
+7 | G. 7
+7 |

| M. 7
+4 |

| N. 6
+7 | O. 0
+7 | P. 2
+7 | Q. 7
+1 | R. 9
+7 | S. 7
+3 |

| T. 8
+7 |

| X. 4
+7 | W. 3
+7 | V. 7
+7 | U. 1
+7 |

A.
| 0 | 7 | 7 | 3 | 1 | 7 |
| + 7 | + 2 | + 4 | + 7 | + 7 | + 6 |

B.
| 7 | 5 | 2 | 9 | 7 | 7 |
| + 8 | + 7 | + 7 | + 7 | + 5 | + 7 |

C.
| 9 | 7 | 1 | 7 | 2 | 3 |
| + 7 | + 0 | + 7 | + 4 | + 7 | + 7 |

D.
| 7 | 7 | 6 | 5 | 7 | 4 |
| + 8 | + 7 | + 7 | + 7 | + 6 | + 7 |

E.
| 1 | 7 | 0 | 8 | 7 | 6 |
| + 7 | + 5 | + 7 | + 7 | + 1 | + 7 |

F.
| 4 | 2 | 7 | 7 | 9 | 7 |
| + 7 | + 7 | + 3 | + 7 | + 7 | + 4 |

G.
| 7 | 8 | 6 | 7 | 7 | 9 |
| + 6 | + 7 | + 7 | + 0 | + 7 | + 7 |

H.
| 3 | 7 | 5 | 2 | 7 | 8 |
| + 7 | + 1 | + 7 | + 7 | + 4 | + 7 |

I.
| 0 | 7 | 6 | 7 | 1 | 7 |
| + 7 | + 2 | + 7 | + 8 | + 7 | + 9 |

J.
| 2 | 7 | 3 | 7 | 7 | 8 |
| + 7 | + 4 | + 7 | + 5 | + 7 | + 7 |

Name: _____ Date: _____

A. 8
   +8

B. 3
   +8

C. 8
   +5

D. 0
   +8

E. 8
   +4

F. 1
   +8

G. 8
   +6

H. 7
   +8

I. 8
   +2

J. 9
   +8

K. 8
   +5

L. 8
   +4

M. 3
   +8

N. 8
   +8

O. 6
   +8

P. 2
   +8

Q. 8
   +7

R. 9
   +8

S. 8
   +0

T. 1
   +8

U. 8
   +2

V. 5
   +8

W. 8
   +3

X. 6
   +8

Y. 0
   +8

Adding 8

Solve each problem. Then, color the picture.

A. 1 + 8 =

B. 8
   + 5

C. 1
   + 8

D. 8
   + 3

E. 2
   + 8

F. 6
   + 8

G. 0
   + 8

H. 8
   + 6

I. 8
   + 3

J. 8
   + 7

K. 8 + 3 =

L. 8
   + 8

M. 2
   + 8

N. 6
   + 8

O. 8
   + 5

P. 8
   + 8

Q. 8 + 9 =

R. 8
   + 4

Adding 8

Solve each problem.

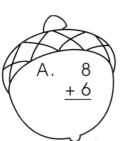 A. 8
   + 6

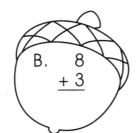 B. 8
   + 3

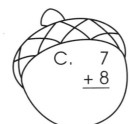 C. 7
   + 8

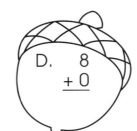 D. 8
   + 0

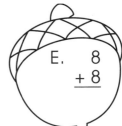 E. 8
   + 8

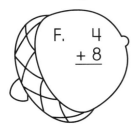 F. 4
   + 8

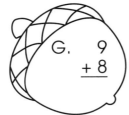 G. 9
   + 8

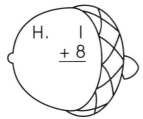 H. 1
   + 8

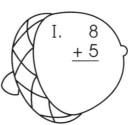 I. 8
   + 5

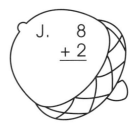 J. 8
   + 2

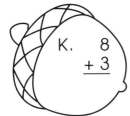 K. 8
   + 3

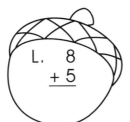 L. 8
   + 5

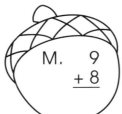 M. 9
   + 8

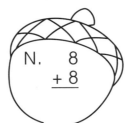 N. 8
   + 8

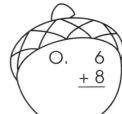 O. 6
   + 8

 P. 8
   + 8

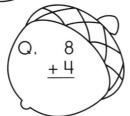 Q. 8
   + 4

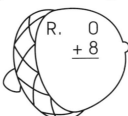 R. 0
   + 8

S. 8
   + 7

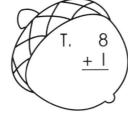 T. 8
   + 1

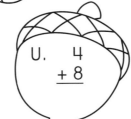 U. 4
   + 8

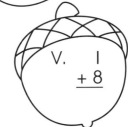 V. 1
   + 8

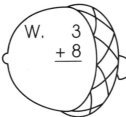 W. 3
   + 8

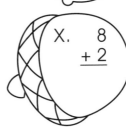 X. 8
   + 2

Y. 6
   + 8

A. $8 + 6 =$ $2 + 8 =$ $0 + 8 =$ $8 + 4 =$ $1 + 8 =$

B. $8 + 3 =$ $8 + 5 =$ $9 + 8 =$ $8 + 7 =$ $8 + 8 =$

C. $3 + 8 =$ $4 + 8 =$ $8 + 2 =$ $8 + 6 =$ $9 + 8 =$

D. $8 + 5 =$ $8 + 8 =$ $0 + 8 =$ $8 + 9 =$ $7 + 8 =$

E. $8 + 2 =$ $5 + 8 =$ $8 + 8 =$ $3 + 8 =$ $8 + 1 =$

F. $8 + 7 =$ $8 + 6 =$ $8 + 0 =$ $8 + 4 =$ $6 + 8 =$

G. $8 + 1 =$ $9 + 8 =$ $8 + 5 =$ $8 + 8 =$ $8 + 0 =$

H. $8 + 2 =$ $6 + 8 =$ $8 + 1 =$ $7 + 8 =$ $8 + 4 =$

I. $9 + 8 =$ $8 + 0 =$ $5 + 8 =$ $8 + 7 =$ $4 + 8 =$

J. $6 + 8 =$ $1 + 8 =$ $8 + 3 =$ $0 + 8 =$ $8 + 2 =$

Name: _____ Date: _____

Adding 9

A.
$$\begin{array}{r} 1 \\ +\ 9 \\ \hline \end{array}$$

B.
$$\begin{array}{r} 9 \\ +\ 5 \\ \hline \end{array}$$

C.
$$\begin{array}{r} 9 \\ +\ 2 \\ \hline \end{array}$$

D.
$$\begin{array}{r} 9 \\ +\ 8 \\ \hline \end{array}$$

E.
$$\begin{array}{r} 3 \\ +\ 9 \\ \hline \end{array}$$

F.
$$\begin{array}{r} 9 \\ +\ 1 \\ \hline \end{array}$$

G.
$$\begin{array}{r} 9 \\ +\ 6 \\ \hline \end{array}$$

H.
$$\begin{array}{r} 2 \\ +\ 9 \\ \hline \end{array}$$

I.
$$\begin{array}{r} 9 \\ +\ 4 \\ \hline \end{array}$$

J.
$$\begin{array}{r} 0 \\ +\ 9 \\ \hline \end{array}$$

K.
$$\begin{array}{r} 9 \\ +\ 5 \\ \hline \end{array}$$

L.
$$\begin{array}{r} 3 \\ +\ 9 \\ \hline \end{array}$$

M.
$$\begin{array}{r} 9 \\ +\ 9 \\ \hline \end{array}$$

N.
$$\begin{array}{r} 4 \\ +\ 9 \\ \hline \end{array}$$

O.
$$\begin{array}{r} 7 \\ +\ 9 \\ \hline \end{array}$$

P.
$$\begin{array}{r} 9 \\ +\ 2 \\ \hline \end{array}$$

Q.
$$\begin{array}{r} 6 \\ +\ 9 \\ \hline \end{array}$$

R.
$$\begin{array}{r} 9 \\ +\ 3 \\ \hline \end{array}$$

S.
$$\begin{array}{r} 9 \\ +\ 0 \\ \hline \end{array}$$

T.
$$\begin{array}{r} 9 \\ +\ 7 \\ \hline \end{array}$$

U.
$$\begin{array}{r} 9 \\ +\ 8 \\ \hline \end{array}$$

V.
$$\begin{array}{r} 9 \\ +\ 3 \\ \hline \end{array}$$

W.
$$\begin{array}{r} 9 \\ +\ 9 \\ \hline \end{array}$$

X.
$$\begin{array}{r} 9 \\ +\ 5 \\ \hline \end{array}$$

Y.
$$\begin{array}{r} 2 \\ +\ 9 \\ \hline \end{array}$$

Adding 9

Solve each problem. Help the mail carrier find the mailbox.

A. 1 +9	B. 9 +7	C. 3 +9	D. 9 +2	E. 9 +6	F. 4 +9

G. 1
+9

M. 9 +4	L. 0 +9	K. 9 +9	J. 9 +8	I. 9 +5	H. 0 +9

N. 7
+9

O. 9 +2	P. 9 +5	Q. 3 +9	R. 9 +6	S. 9 +9	T. 9 +8

U. 0
+9

Y. 9 +9	X. 9 +2	W. 7 +9	V. 9 +4

Adding 9

Solve each problem. Then, color the picture.

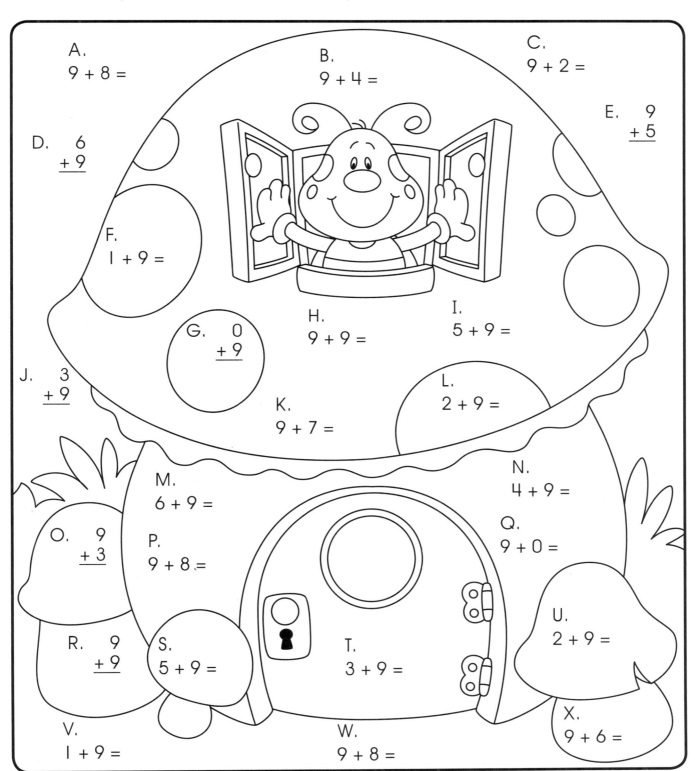

A.
9 + 8 =

B.
9 + 4 =

C.
9 + 2 =

E.   9
    + 5

D.   6
    + 9

F.
1 + 9 =

G.   0
    + 9

H.
9 + 9 =

I.
5 + 9 =

J.   3
    + 9

K.
9 + 7 =

L.
2 + 9 =

M.
6 + 9 =

N.
4 + 9 =

O.   9
    + 3

P.
9 + 8 =

Q.
9 + 0 =

R.   9
    + 9

S.
5 + 9 =

T.
3 + 9 =

U.
2 + 9 =

V.
1 + 9 =

W.
9 + 8 =

X.
9 + 6 =

1 2 3 4 5
Minutes

Adding 9

Score

A. 9 + 9	9 + 5	9 + 0	9 + 3	2 + 9
B. 6 + 9	9 + 8	4 + 9	9 + 7	9 + 1
C. 9 + 3	9 + 6	9 + 9	0 + 9	1 + 9
D. 2 + 9	9 + 4	5 + 9	9 + 8	7 + 9
E. 9 + 2	1 + 9	9 + 0	9 + 9	9 + 7
F. 5 + 9	9 + 3	9 + 8	9 + 4	6 + 9
G. 2 + 9	7 + 9	0 + 9	9 + 9	3 + 9
H. 9 + 4	9 + 5	6 + 9	9 + 8	9 + 0
I. 9 + 6	9 + 7	9 + 3	9 + 0	5 + 9
J. 9 + 9	4 + 9	9 + 1	9 + 2	8 + 9

Adding 7, 8, and 9

Score

A.
$$0 + 7$$ $$7 + 5$$ $$8 + 0$$ $$9 + 7$$ $$3 + 9$$ $$9 + 8$$

B.
$$7 + 6$$ $$4 + 7$$ $$9 + 5$$ $$7 + 2$$ $$8 + 9$$ $$8 + 6$$

C.
$$0 + 9$$ $$7 + 5$$ $$3 + 7$$ $$8 + 5$$ $$4 + 7$$ $$9 + 2$$

D.
$$8 + 7$$ $$9 + 6$$ $$7 + 7$$ $$8 + 3$$ $$9 + 9$$ $$7 + 6$$

E.
$$7 + 9$$ $$7 + 5$$ $$8 + 0$$ $$1 + 9$$ $$9 + 8$$ $$9 + 4$$

F.
$$2 + 9$$ $$8 + 5$$ $$7 + 4$$ $$6 + 9$$ $$8 + 8$$ $$5 + 9$$

G.
$$8 + 4$$ $$9 + 3$$ $$2 + 7$$ $$9 + 2$$ $$8 + 8$$ $$8 + 6$$

H.
$$7 + 9$$ $$0 + 8$$ $$7 + 5$$ $$3 + 7$$ $$9 + 4$$ $$6 + 9$$

I.
$$8 + 2$$ $$0 + 9$$ $$2 + 9$$ $$8 + 1$$ $$7 + 0$$ $$2 + 9$$

J.
$$5 + 8$$ $$8 + 9$$ $$8 + 7$$ $$4 + 7$$ $$8 + 3$$ $$1 + 7$$

Name: _____   Date: _____

Adding 7, 8, and 9

Solve each problem. Circle each problem and answer in the puzzle.
Problems can be hidden across or down. The first one has been done
for you.

A.   6 + 9 = **15**   8 + 9 =   7 + 8 =   5 + 8 =   2 + 8 =

B.   4 + 9 =   9 + 7 =   1 + 9 =   5 + 9 =   6 + 8 =

Name: _____ Date: _____

Subtracting 1

A. 10
    − 1

B. 5
    − 1

C. 2
    − 1

D. 8
    − 1

E. 3
    − 1

F. 9
    − 1

G. 6
    − 1

H. 2
    − 1

I. 4
    − 1

J. 6
    − 1

K. 5
    − 1

L. 3
    − 1

M. 9
    − 1

N. 8
    − 1

O. 7
    − 1

P. 2
    − 1

Q. 6
    − 1

R. 1
    − 1

S. 4
    − 1

T. 9
    − 1

U. 8
    − 1

V. 3
    − 1

W. 9
    − 1

X. 5
    − 1

Y. 2
    − 1

Subtracting 1

Solve each problem.

A.
$$\begin{array}{r}1\\-1\\\hline\end{array}$$
$$\begin{array}{r}7\\-1\\\hline\end{array}$$
$$\begin{array}{r}3\\-1\\\hline\end{array}$$
$$\begin{array}{r}2\\-1\\\hline\end{array}$$
$$\begin{array}{r}6\\-1\\\hline\end{array}$$

B.
$$\begin{array}{r}4\\-1\\\hline\end{array}$$
$$\begin{array}{r}9\\-1\\\hline\end{array}$$
$$\begin{array}{r}4\\-1\\\hline\end{array}$$
$$\begin{array}{r}5\\-1\\\hline\end{array}$$
$$\begin{array}{r}8\\-1\\\hline\end{array}$$

C.
$$\begin{array}{r}9\\-1\\\hline\end{array}$$
$$\begin{array}{r}6\\-1\\\hline\end{array}$$
$$\begin{array}{r}4\\-1\\\hline\end{array}$$
$$\begin{array}{r}7\\-1\\\hline\end{array}$$
$$\begin{array}{r}2\\-1\\\hline\end{array}$$

D.
$$\begin{array}{r}5\\-1\\\hline\end{array}$$
$$\begin{array}{r}3\\-1\\\hline\end{array}$$
$$\begin{array}{r}6\\-1\\\hline\end{array}$$
$$\begin{array}{r}10\\-1\\\hline\end{array}$$

E.
$$\begin{array}{r}8\\-1\\\hline\end{array}$$
$$\begin{array}{r}2\\-1\\\hline\end{array}$$
$$\begin{array}{r}4\\-1\\\hline\end{array}$$

F.
$$\begin{array}{r}7\\-1\\\hline\end{array}$$
$$\begin{array}{r}2\\-1\\\hline\end{array}$$
$$\begin{array}{r}9\\-1\\\hline\end{array}$$

Subtracting 1

Solve each problem. Help the boy find the school.

A. 8
−1

B. 4
−1

C. 2
−1

D. 6
−1

E. 10
−1

F. 5
−1

J. 7
−1

I. 9
−1

H. 6
−1

G. 3
−1

K. 2
−1

L. 5
−1

M. 3
−1

N. 6
−1

O. 8
−1

P. 7
−1

Q. 4
−1

T. 9
−1

S. 1
−1

R. 10
−1

A. $\begin{array}{r} 1 \\ -1 \\ \hline \end{array}$ $\qquad$ $\begin{array}{r} 5 \\ -1 \\ \hline \end{array}$ $\qquad$ $\begin{array}{r} 6 \\ -1 \\ \hline \end{array}$ $\qquad$ $\begin{array}{r} 3 \\ -1 \\ \hline \end{array}$ $\qquad$ $\begin{array}{r} 2 \\ -1 \\ \hline \end{array}$

B. $\begin{array}{r} 6 \\ -1 \\ \hline \end{array}$ $\qquad$ $\begin{array}{r} 8 \\ -1 \\ \hline \end{array}$ $\qquad$ $\begin{array}{r} 4 \\ -1 \\ \hline \end{array}$ $\qquad$ $\begin{array}{r} 7 \\ -1 \\ \hline \end{array}$ $\qquad$ $\begin{array}{r} 9 \\ -1 \\ \hline \end{array}$

C. $\begin{array}{r} 3 \\ -1 \\ \hline \end{array}$ $\qquad$ $\begin{array}{r} 6 \\ -1 \\ \hline \end{array}$ $\qquad$ $\begin{array}{r} 9 \\ -1 \\ \hline \end{array}$ $\qquad$ $\begin{array}{r} 7 \\ -1 \\ \hline \end{array}$ $\qquad$ $\begin{array}{r} 1 \\ -1 \\ \hline \end{array}$

D. $\begin{array}{r} 2 \\ -1 \\ \hline \end{array}$ $\qquad$ $\begin{array}{r} 4 \\ -1 \\ \hline \end{array}$ $\qquad$ $\begin{array}{r} 5 \\ -1 \\ \hline \end{array}$ $\qquad$ $\begin{array}{r} 8 \\ -1 \\ \hline \end{array}$ $\qquad$ $\begin{array}{r} 7 \\ -1 \\ \hline \end{array}$

E. $\begin{array}{r} 2 \\ -1 \\ \hline \end{array}$ $\qquad$ $\begin{array}{r} 9 \\ -1 \\ \hline \end{array}$ $\qquad$ $\begin{array}{r} 4 \\ -1 \\ \hline \end{array}$ $\qquad$ $\begin{array}{r} 1 \\ -1 \\ \hline \end{array}$ $\qquad$ $\begin{array}{r} 7 \\ -1 \\ \hline \end{array}$

F. $\begin{array}{r} 5 \\ -1 \\ \hline \end{array}$ $\qquad$ $\begin{array}{r} 3 \\ -1 \\ \hline \end{array}$ $\qquad$ $\begin{array}{r} 8 \\ -1 \\ \hline \end{array}$ $\qquad$ $\begin{array}{r} 4 \\ -1 \\ \hline \end{array}$ $\qquad$ $\begin{array}{r} 6 \\ -1 \\ \hline \end{array}$

G. $\begin{array}{r} 4 \\ -1 \\ \hline \end{array}$ $\qquad$ $\begin{array}{r} 7 \\ -1 \\ \hline \end{array}$ $\qquad$ $\begin{array}{r} 9 \\ -1 \\ \hline \end{array}$ $\qquad$ $\begin{array}{r} 2 \\ -1 \\ \hline \end{array}$ $\qquad$ $\begin{array}{r} 3 \\ -1 \\ \hline \end{array}$

H. $\begin{array}{r} 2 \\ -1 \\ \hline \end{array}$ $\qquad$ $\begin{array}{r} 5 \\ -1 \\ \hline \end{array}$ $\qquad$ $\begin{array}{r} 6 \\ -1 \\ \hline \end{array}$ $\qquad$ $\begin{array}{r} 8 \\ -1 \\ \hline \end{array}$ $\qquad$ $\begin{array}{r} 1 \\ -1 \\ \hline \end{array}$

I. $\begin{array}{r} 6 \\ -1 \\ \hline \end{array}$ $\qquad$ $\begin{array}{r} 7 \\ -1 \\ \hline \end{array}$ $\qquad$ $\begin{array}{r} 3 \\ -1 \\ \hline \end{array}$ $\qquad$ $\begin{array}{r} 4 \\ -1 \\ \hline \end{array}$ $\qquad$ $\begin{array}{r} 5 \\ -1 \\ \hline \end{array}$

J. $\begin{array}{r} 1 \\ -1 \\ \hline \end{array}$ $\qquad$ $\begin{array}{r} 4 \\ -1 \\ \hline \end{array}$ $\qquad$ $\begin{array}{r} 9 \\ -1 \\ \hline \end{array}$ $\qquad$ $\begin{array}{r} 2 \\ -1 \\ \hline \end{array}$ $\qquad$ $\begin{array}{r} 8 \\ -1 \\ \hline \end{array}$

Name: _____ Date: _____

A. 3
   −2

B. 4
   −2

C. 2
   −2

D. 6
   −2

E. 8
   −2

F. 5
   −2

G. 3
   −2

H. 8
   −2

I. 9
   −2

J. 7
   −2

K. 11
   −2

L. 5
   −2

M. 7
   −2

N. 3
   −2

O. 8
   −2

P. 6
   −2

Q. 4
   −2

R. 9
   −2

S. 4
   −2

T. 10
   −2

U. 3
   −2

V. 6
   −2

W. 8
   −2

X. 2
   −2

Y. 5
   −2

Subtracting 2

Solve each problem. Then, color the picture.

A. 4
  − 2

B. 7
  − 2

C. 5
  − 2

D. 9
  − 2

E. 6
  − 2

F. 11
  − 2

G. 3
  − 2

H. 5
  − 2

I. 8
  − 2

J. 4
  − 2

K. 8
  − 2

L. 9
  − 2

M. 6
  − 2

N. 2
  − 2

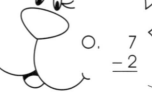

O. 7
  − 2

P. 4
  − 2

Q. 9
  − 2

R. 5
  − 2

S. 10
  − 2

Y. 11
  − 2

T. 8
  − 2

U. 9
  − 2

V. 4
  − 2

W. 8
  − 2

X. 2
  − 2

Name: _____ Date: _____

Subtracting 2

Solve each problem.

A. 4 − 2 =

B. 7 − 2 =

C. 3 − 2 =

D. 10 − 2 =

E. 5 − 2 =

F. 9 − 2 =

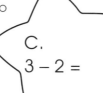

G. 2 − 2 =

H. 4 − 2 =

I. 2 − 2 =

J. 5 − 2 =

K. 7 − 2 =

L. 2 − 2 =

M. 5 − 2 =

N. 4 − 2 =

O. 6 − 2 =

P. 8 − 2 =

Q. 7 − 2 =

R. 11 − 2 =

T. 5 − 2 =

U. 9 − 2 =

V. 3 − 2 =

S. 10 − 2 =

Y. 6 − 2 =

W. 5 − 2 =

X. 7 − 2 =

Name: _____   Date: _____

Subtracting 2

Score

A.	7 – 2 =	2 – 2 =	4 – 2 =	3 – 2 =	11 – 2 =
B.	6 – 2 =	8 – 2 =	5 – 2 =	10 – 2 =	9 – 2 =
C.	5 – 2 =	10 – 2 =	9 – 2 =	11 – 2 =	6 – 2 =
D.	4 – 2 =	2 – 2 =	3 – 2 =	8 – 2 =	7 – 2 =
E.	2 – 2 =	9 – 2 =	3 – 2 =	4 – 2 =	7 – 2 =
F.	5 – 2 =	8 – 2 =	11 – 2 =	9 – 2 =	6 – 2 =
G.	4 – 2 =	7 – 2 =	3 – 2 =	6 – 2 =	10 – 2 =
H.	2 – 2 =	5 – 2 =	8 – 2 =	9 – 2 =	11 – 2 =
I.	4 – 2 =	11 – 2 =	3 – 2 =	6 – 2 =	10 – 2 =
J.	9 – 2 =	5 – 2 =	8 – 2 =	2 – 2 =	7 – 2 =

Name: _____ Date: _____

A. 3
   − 3

B. 8
   − 3

C. 5
   − 3

D. 9
   − 3

E. 4
   − 3

F. 6
   − 3

G. 9
   − 3

H. 7
   − 3

I. 3
   − 3

J. 11
   − 3

K. 5
   − 3

L. 4
   − 3

M. 8
   − 3

N. 3
   − 3

O. 6
   − 3

P. 4
   − 3

Q. 12
   − 3

R. 9
   − 3

S. 8
   − 3

T. 7
   − 3

U. 6
   − 3

V. 5
   − 3

W. 10
   − 3

X. 6
   − 3

Y. 8
   − 3

Subtracting 3

Solve each problem. Help the rabbit find the pool.

A. 9
  −3

B. 11
  −3

C. 6
  −3

D. 4
  −3

E. 8
  −3

F. 4
  −3

G. 3
  −3

H. 7
  −3

I. 9
  −3

M. 7
  −3

L. 8
  −3

K. 5
  −3

J. 10
  −3

N. 9
  −3

O. 11
  −3

P. 7
  −3

Q. 9
  −3

R. 12
  −3

S. 7
  −3

T. 5
  −3

Subtracting 3

Solve each problem. Then, color the picture.

A.
6 – 3 =

B.
10 – 3 =

C.
7 – 3 =

D.   4
    – 3

E.
11 – 3 =

F.
12 – 3 =

G.
5 – 3 =

H.
9 – 3 =

I.
6 – 3 =

J.
10 – 3 =

K.
7 – 3 =

L.   5
    – 3

M.
9 – 3 =

N.
3 – 3 =

O.
6 – 3 =

P.   8
    – 3

Q.
7 – 3 =

R.   5
    – 3

S.
4 – 3 =

T.
9 – 3 =

Y.
12 – 3 =

U.
4 – 3 =

V.
6 – 3 =

W.
8 – 3 =

X.
7 – 3 =

Subtracting 3

Score

A.	6 − 3	10 − 3	9 − 3	4 − 3	11 − 3
B.	3 − 3	5 − 3	12 − 3	7 − 3	8 − 3
C.	5 − 3	4 − 3	6 − 3	11 − 3	12 − 3
D.	9 − 3	3 − 3	8 − 3	10 − 3	7 − 3
E.	6 − 3	5 − 3	12 − 3	10 − 3	8 − 3
F.	7 − 3	4 − 3	9 − 3	4 − 3	11 − 3
G.	10 − 3	9 − 3	5 − 3	12 − 3	11 − 3
H.	6 − 3	8 − 3	3 − 3	7 − 3	4 − 3
I.	9 − 3	8 − 3	5 − 3	12 − 3	4 − 3
J.	3 − 3	10 − 3	7 − 3	11 − 3	6 − 3

Subtracting 1, 2, and 3

Score

| 1 | 2 | 3 | 4 | 5 |
Minutes

A.
$$\begin{array}{r} 10 \\ -1 \\ \hline \end{array}$$
$$\begin{array}{r} 5 \\ -1 \\ \hline \end{array}$$
$$\begin{array}{r} 9 \\ -2 \\ \hline \end{array}$$
$$\begin{array}{r} 3 \\ -1 \\ \hline \end{array}$$
$$\begin{array}{r} 4 \\ -2 \\ \hline \end{array}$$
$$\begin{array}{r} 9 \\ -2 \\ \hline \end{array}$$

B.
$$\begin{array}{r} 6 \\ -1 \\ \hline \end{array}$$
$$\begin{array}{r} 11 \\ -3 \\ \hline \end{array}$$
$$\begin{array}{r} 5 \\ -3 \\ \hline \end{array}$$
$$\begin{array}{r} 9 \\ -1 \\ \hline \end{array}$$
$$\begin{array}{r} 8 \\ -3 \\ \hline \end{array}$$
$$\begin{array}{r} 6 \\ -2 \\ \hline \end{array}$$

C.
$$\begin{array}{r} 11 \\ -3 \\ \hline \end{array}$$
$$\begin{array}{r} 5 \\ -1 \\ \hline \end{array}$$
$$\begin{array}{r} 1 \\ -1 \\ \hline \end{array}$$
$$\begin{array}{r} 5 \\ -2 \\ \hline \end{array}$$
$$\begin{array}{r} 4 \\ -1 \\ \hline \end{array}$$
$$\begin{array}{r} 5 \\ -3 \\ \hline \end{array}$$

D.
$$\begin{array}{r} 8 \\ -1 \\ \hline \end{array}$$
$$\begin{array}{r} 11 \\ -2 \\ \hline \end{array}$$
$$\begin{array}{r} 2 \\ -1 \\ \hline \end{array}$$
$$\begin{array}{r} 9 \\ -3 \\ \hline \end{array}$$
$$\begin{array}{r} 9 \\ -1 \\ \hline \end{array}$$
$$\begin{array}{r} 6 \\ -1 \\ \hline \end{array}$$

E.
$$\begin{array}{r} 7 \\ -3 \\ \hline \end{array}$$
$$\begin{array}{r} 5 \\ -1 \\ \hline \end{array}$$
$$\begin{array}{r} 3 \\ -2 \\ \hline \end{array}$$
$$\begin{array}{r} 8 \\ -3 \\ \hline \end{array}$$
$$\begin{array}{r} 9 \\ -2 \\ \hline \end{array}$$
$$\begin{array}{r} 10 \\ -3 \\ \hline \end{array}$$

F.
$$\begin{array}{r} 3 \\ -3 \\ \hline \end{array}$$
$$\begin{array}{r} 11 \\ -3 \\ \hline \end{array}$$
$$\begin{array}{r} 4 \\ -1 \\ \hline \end{array}$$
$$\begin{array}{r} 6 \\ -3 \\ \hline \end{array}$$
$$\begin{array}{r} 2 \\ -2 \\ \hline \end{array}$$
$$\begin{array}{r} 8 \\ -3 \\ \hline \end{array}$$

G.
$$\begin{array}{r} 9 \\ -2 \\ \hline \end{array}$$
$$\begin{array}{r} 4 \\ -3 \\ \hline \end{array}$$
$$\begin{array}{r} 2 \\ -1 \\ \hline \end{array}$$
$$\begin{array}{r} 9 \\ -3 \\ \hline \end{array}$$
$$\begin{array}{r} 8 \\ -2 \\ \hline \end{array}$$
$$\begin{array}{r} 10 \\ -2 \\ \hline \end{array}$$

H.
$$\begin{array}{r} 3 \\ -1 \\ \hline \end{array}$$
$$\begin{array}{r} 9 \\ -2 \\ \hline \end{array}$$
$$\begin{array}{r} 5 \\ -1 \\ \hline \end{array}$$
$$\begin{array}{r} 2 \\ -1 \\ \hline \end{array}$$
$$\begin{array}{r} 12 \\ -3 \\ \hline \end{array}$$
$$\begin{array}{r} 6 \\ -3 \\ \hline \end{array}$$

I.
$$\begin{array}{r} 5 \\ -2 \\ \hline \end{array}$$
$$\begin{array}{r} 3 \\ -1 \\ \hline \end{array}$$
$$\begin{array}{r} 9 \\ -1 \\ \hline \end{array}$$
$$\begin{array}{r} 2 \\ -2 \\ \hline \end{array}$$
$$\begin{array}{r} 11 \\ -3 \\ \hline \end{array}$$
$$\begin{array}{r} 9 \\ -1 \\ \hline \end{array}$$

J.
$$\begin{array}{r} 10 \\ -2 \\ \hline \end{array}$$
$$\begin{array}{r} 8 \\ -1 \\ \hline \end{array}$$
$$\begin{array}{r} 6 \\ -3 \\ \hline \end{array}$$
$$\begin{array}{r} 4 \\ -3 \\ \hline \end{array}$$
$$\begin{array}{r} 11 \\ -2 \\ \hline \end{array}$$
$$\begin{array}{r} 9 \\ -3 \\ \hline \end{array}$$

Subtracting 1, 2, and 3

Solve each problem. Circle each problem and answer in the puzzle. Problems can be hidden across or down. The first one has been done for you.

A. $4 - 3 = 1$ $3 - 2 =$ $5 - 3 =$ $7 - 2 =$ $3 - 3 =$

B. $8 - 3 =$ $6 - 3 =$ $4 - 2 =$ $5 - 1 =$ $8 - 1 =$

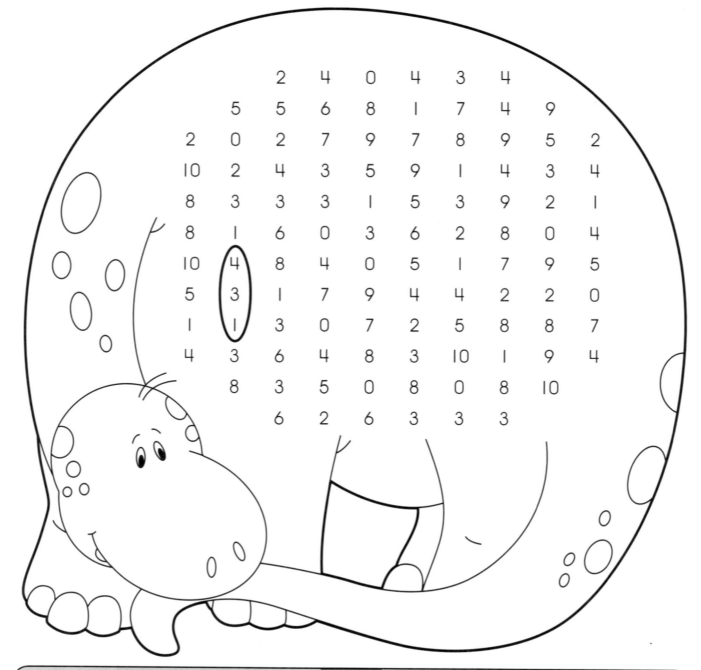

Name: _____ Date: _____

Subtracting 1, 2, and 3

Solve each problem. Then, use the color key to color the picture.

Color Key

2 = yellow   4 = gray   6 = blue

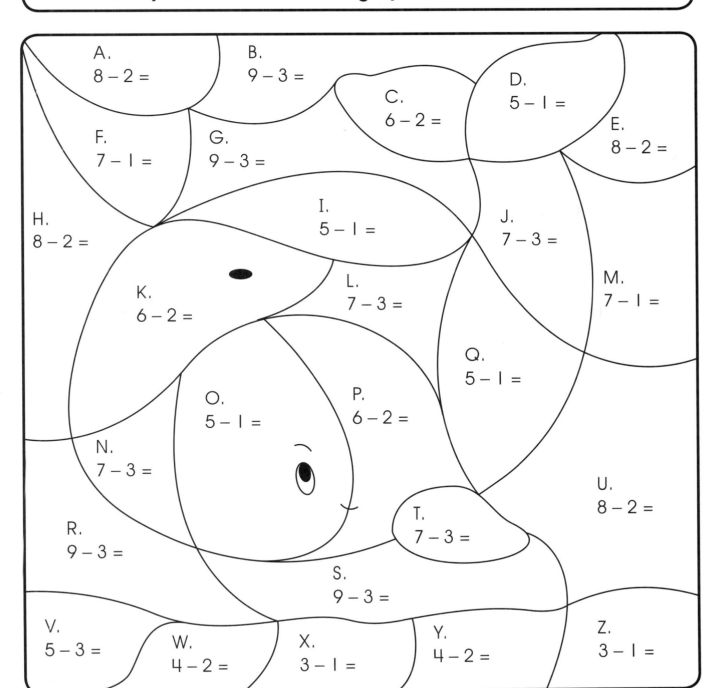

A.
8 – 2 =

B.
9 – 3 =

C.
6 – 2 =

D.
5 – 1 =

E.
8 – 2 =

F.
7 – 1 =

G.
9 – 3 =

H.
8 – 2 =

I.
5 – 1 =

J.
7 – 3 =

K.
6 – 2 =

L.
7 – 3 =

M.
7 – 1 =

Q.
5 – 1 =

N.
7 – 3 =

O.
5 – 1 =

P.
6 – 2 =

R.
9 – 3 =

T.
7 – 3 =

U.
8 – 2 =

S.
9 – 3 =

V.
5 – 3 =

W.
4 – 2 =

X.
3 – 1 =

Y.
4 – 2 =

Z.
3 – 1 =

1 2 3 4 5
Minutes

Subtracting 1, 2, and 3

Score

A.	3 −1	5 −2	10 −1	8 −1	10 −2	6 −2
B.	9 −1	6 −3	7 −2	9 −3	4 −3	11 −2
C.	5 −1	8 −3	6 −1	9 −2	4 −1	5 −3
D.	2 −2	10 −2	4 −3	7 −2	8 −1	11 −3
E.	9 −2	8 −1	6 −3	4 −2	8 −2	6 −1
F.	10 −1	7 −2	9 −3	2 −1	4 −2	7 −3
G.	5 −1	12 −3	10 −1	11 −2	6 −3	7 −1
H.	8 −3	6 −3	2 −2	8 −1	4 −2	9 −1
I.	10 −1	3 −2	9 −1	5 −1	3 −1	2 −1
J.	2 −2	6 −1	8 −3	11 −2	7 −3	4 −3

Name: _____ Date: _____

Subtracting 4

1 2 3 4 5
Minutes

A.
$\begin{array}{r} 7 \\ -4 \\ \hline \end{array}$

B.
$\begin{array}{r} 12 \\ -4 \\ \hline \end{array}$

C.
$\begin{array}{r} 5 \\ -4 \\ \hline \end{array}$

D.
$\begin{array}{r} 6 \\ -4 \\ \hline \end{array}$

E.
$\begin{array}{r} 8 \\ -4 \\ \hline \end{array}$

F.
$\begin{array}{r} 10 \\ -4 \\ \hline \end{array}$

G.
$\begin{array}{r} 6 \\ -4 \\ \hline \end{array}$

H.
$\begin{array}{r} 11 \\ -4 \\ \hline \end{array}$

I.
$\begin{array}{r} 7 \\ -4 \\ \hline \end{array}$

J.
$\begin{array}{r} 4 \\ -4 \\ \hline \end{array}$

K.
$\begin{array}{r} 9 \\ -4 \\ \hline \end{array}$

L.
$\begin{array}{r} 13 \\ -4 \\ \hline \end{array}$

M.
$\begin{array}{r} 6 \\ -4 \\ \hline \end{array}$

N.
$\begin{array}{r} 9 \\ -4 \\ \hline \end{array}$

O.
$\begin{array}{r} 10 \\ -4 \\ \hline \end{array}$

P.
$\begin{array}{r} 5 \\ -4 \\ \hline \end{array}$

Q.
$\begin{array}{r} 13 \\ -4 \\ \hline \end{array}$

R.
$\begin{array}{r} 4 \\ -4 \\ \hline \end{array}$

S.
$\begin{array}{r} 8 \\ -4 \\ \hline \end{array}$

T.
$\begin{array}{r} 9 \\ -4 \\ \hline \end{array}$

U.
$\begin{array}{r} 6 \\ -4 \\ \hline \end{array}$

V.
$\begin{array}{r} 5 \\ -4 \\ \hline \end{array}$

W.
$\begin{array}{r} 11 \\ -4 \\ \hline \end{array}$

X.
$\begin{array}{r} 10 \\ -4 \\ \hline \end{array}$

Y.
$\begin{array}{r} 4 \\ -4 \\ \hline \end{array}$

Subtracting 4

Solve each problem.

A. 12
  − 4

B. 4
  − 4

C. 13
  − 4

D. 9
  − 4

E. 10
  − 4

F. 8
  − 4

G. 9
  − 4

H. 5
  − 4

I. 6
  − 4

J. 7
  − 4

K. 9
  − 4

L. 10
  − 4

M. 11
  − 4

N. 4
  − 4

O. 7
  − 4

P. 9
  − 4

Q. 13
  − 4

R. 6
  − 4

S. 9
  − 4

T. 11
  − 4

U. 4
  − 4

V. 12
  − 4

W. 7
  − 4

X. 6
  − 4

Y. 13
  − 4

Name: _____ Date: _____

Subtracting 4

Solve each problem. Help the family find their home.

A.
7 – 4 =

B.
4 – 4 =

C.
12 – 4 =

D.
6 – 4 =

E.
11 – 4 =

F.
5 – 4 =

G.
13 – 4 =

H.
10 – 4 =

I.
9 – 4 =

J.
7 – 4 =

K.
8 – 4 =

L.
5 – 4 =

M.
13 – 4 =

N.
6 – 4 =

O.
12 – 4 =

P.
7 – 4 =

Q.
4 – 4 =

R.
10 – 4 =

S.
11 – 4 =

T.
9 – 4 =

1 2 3 4 5
Minutes

Subtracting 4

Score

A. 8   12   9   5   6
   −4   −4   −4   −4   −4

B. 11   10   7   13   4
   −4   −4   −4   −4   −4

C. 6   9   13   10   5
   −4   −4   −4   −4   −4

D. 8   7   10   4   11
   −4   −4   −4   −4   −4

E. 12   6   7   10   9
   −4   −4   −4   −4   −4

F. 4   8   5   11   13
   −4   −4   −4   −4   −4

G. 13   7   9   8   12
   −4   −4   −4   −4   −4

H. 6   4   11   5   10
   −4   −4   −4   −4   −4

I. 4   7   13   11   12
   −4   −4   −4   −4   −4

J. 5   10   8   9   6
   −4   −4   −4   −4   −4

Name: _____ Date: _____

A. 10
   − 5

B. 9
   − 5

C. 12
   − 5

D. 8
   − 5

E. 6
   − 5

F. 9
   − 5

G. 5
   − 5

H. 14
   − 5

I. 13
   − 5

J. 10
   − 5

K. 12
   − 5

L. 10
   − 5

M. 9
   − 5

N. 14
   − 5

O. 7
   − 5

P. 5
   − 5

Q. 10
   − 5

R. 5
   − 5

S. 8
   − 5

T. 6
   − 5

U. 7
   − 5

V. 8
   − 5

W. 14
   − 5

X. 7
   − 5

Y. 11
   − 5

Subtracting 5

Solve each problem. Then, color the picture.

A. 11
   − 5

B. 7
   − 5

C. 13
   − 5

D. 12
   − 5

E. 6
   − 5

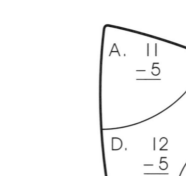

F. 14
   − 5

G. 9
   − 5

M. 8
   − 5

H. 10
   − 5

L. 11
   − 5

K. 14
   − 5

P. 12
   − 5

J. 10
   − 5

O. 7
   − 5

I. 9
   − 5

N. 5
   − 5

U. 13
   − 5

V. 6
   − 5

S. 8
   − 5

T. 10
   − 5

Q. 14
   − 5

R. 11
   − 5

W. 7
   − 5

X. 12
   − 5

Y. 9
   − 5

Name: _____   Date: _____

Subtracting 5

Solve each problem.

A. 8 – 5 =   14 – 5 =   12 – 5 =   6 – 5 =

B. 5 – 5 =   7 – 5 =   13 – 5 =   10 – 5 =

C. 9 – 5 =   7 – 5 =   12 – 5 =   5 – 5 =

D. 13 – 5 =   6 – 5 =   8 – 5 =   7 – 5 =

E. 14 – 5 =   10 – 5 =   5 – 5 =

F. 9 – 5 =   5 – 5 =

G. 13 – 5 =   8 – 5 =

H. 12 – 5 =   6 – 5 =

Name: _____ Date: _____

Subtracting 5

Score

A.　9 − 5 =　　　5 − 5 =　　　10 − 5 =　　　13 − 5 =　　　12 − 5 =

B.　6 − 5 =　　　8 − 5 =　　　14 − 5 =　　　7 − 5 =　　　11 − 5 =

C.　13 − 5 =　　　6 − 5 =　　　9 − 5 =　　　10 − 5 =　　　5 − 5 =

D.　7 − 5 =　　　14 − 5 =　　　11 − 5 =　　　8 − 5 =　　　12 − 5 =

E.　12 − 5 =　　　9 − 5 =　　　10 − 5 =　　　5 − 5 =　　　7 − 5 =

F.　11 − 5 =　　　13 − 5 =　　　8 − 5 =　　　14 − 5 =　　　6 − 5 =

G.　14 − 5 =　　　7 − 5 =　　　9 − 5 =　　　11 − 5 =　　　13 − 5 =

H.　12 − 5 =　　　5 − 5 =　　　6 − 5 =　　　8 − 5 =　　　10 − 5 =

I.　6 − 5 =　　　11 − 5 =　　　13 − 5 =　　　10 − 5 =　　　5 − 5 =

J.　8 − 5 =　　　14 − 5 =　　　9 − 5 =　　　12 − 5 =　　　7 − 5 =

Subtracting 6

A. 10
    − 6

B. 14
    − 6

C. 12
    − 6

D. 6
    − 6

E. 11
    − 6

F. 15
    − 6

G. 13
    − 6

H. 8
    − 6

I. 9
    − 6

J. 7
    − 6

K. 6
    − 6

L. 15
    − 6

M. 7
    − 6

N. 13
    − 6

O. 8
    − 6

P. 12
    − 6

Q. 14
    − 6

R. 10
    − 6

S. 11
    − 6

T. 9
    − 6

U. 13
    − 6

V. 12
    − 6

W. 8
    − 6

X. 6
    − 6

Y. 15
    − 6

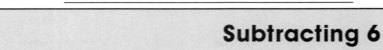

Subtracting 6

Solve each problem. Help the kitten find the easel.

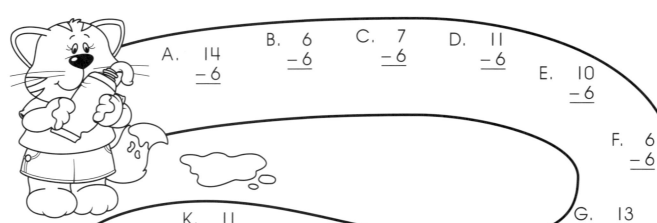

A. 14
   – 6

B. 6
   – 6

C. 7
   – 6

D. 11
   – 6

E. 10
   – 6

F. 6
   – 6

G. 13
   – 6

H. 8
   – 6

I. 15
   – 6

J. 9
   – 6

K. 11
   – 6

L. 6
   – 6

M. 9
   – 6

N. 7
   – 6

O. 8
   – 6

P. 14
   – 6

Q. 9
   – 6

R. 15
   – 6

S. 10
   – 6

T. 13
   – 6

U. 10
   – 6

V. 14
   – 6

W. 8
   – 6

X. 6
   – 6

Y. 9
   – 6

Subtracting 6

Solve each problem. Then, color the picture.

A.
7 − 6 =

B.
8 − 6 =

C.
10 − 6 =

D.
13 − 6 =

E.
15 − 6 =

F.
9 − 6 =

G.
14 − 6 =

H.
11 − 6 =

I.
6 − 6 =

J.
9 − 6 =

K.
14 − 6 =

L.
11 − 6 =

M.
15 − 6 =

N.
14 − 6 =

Q.
6 − 6 =

O.
10 − 6 =

P.
7 − 6 =

T.
11 − 6 =

R.
9 − 6 =

S.
13 − 6 =

W.
15 − 6 =

U.
13 − 6 =

V.
6 − 6 =

X.
11 − 6 =

Y.
7 − 6 =

1 2 3 4 5
Minutes

Subtracting 6

Score

A.	10 − 6	7 − 6	14 − 6	13 − 6	11 − 6
B.	6 − 6	8 − 6	15 − 6	12 − 6	9 − 6
C.	15 − 6	6 − 6	9 − 6	10 − 6	11 − 6
D.	14 − 6	12 − 6	13 − 6	8 − 6	7 − 6
E.	6 − 6	9 − 6	13 − 6	14 − 6	7 − 6
F.	15 − 6	10 − 6	8 − 6	11 − 6	12 − 6
G.	14 − 6	7 − 6	13 − 6	6 − 6	9 − 6
H.	11 − 6	15 − 6	8 − 6	12 − 6	10 − 6
I.	6 − 6	9 − 6	13 − 6	11 − 6	15 − 6
J.	10 − 6	14 − 6	8 − 6	6 − 6	12 − 6

Name: _____ Date: _____

A. 10 −5	13 −5	10 −4	7 −6	14 −6	9 −4
B. 6 −5	4 −4	12 −5	9 −5	8 −6	6 −4
C. 9 −5	7 −5	12 −5	13 −6	7 −5	15 −6
D. 8 −5	13 −4	14 −5	9 −6	10 −5	6 −5
E. 7 −6	5 −5	10 −6	6 −4	11 −4	6 −5
F. 12 −6	10 −5	14 −5	6 −6	7 −4	8 −6
G. 11 −4	6 −4	14 −5	10 −5	9 −5	6 −4
H. 6 −5	10 −4	5 −4	15 −6	7 −6	8 −4
I. 6 −5	13 −4	14 −5	11 −4	8 −4	5 −4
J. 14 −5	13 −5	8 −6	7 −4	9 −5	10 −6

Subtracting 4, 5, and 6

Solve each problem. Circle each problem and answer in the puzzle. Problems can be hidden across or down. The first one has been done for you.

A. $6 - 4 =$ **2** $12 - 6 =$ $7 - 4 =$ $12 - 5 =$

B. $13 - 5 =$ $13 - 6 =$ $8 - 6 =$ $10 - 5 =$

C. $10 - 6 =$ $11 - 4 =$ $9 - 5 =$ $8 - 4 =$

Subtracting 1–6

Solve each problem. Draw a line from each apple to the bug with the matching answer.

A.
6 − 5 =

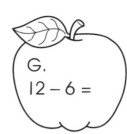 **7**

G.
12 − 6 =

 **8**

B.
10 − 3 =

 **0**

H.
10 − 2 =

 **6**

C.
5 − 5 =

 **1**

I.
5 − 3 =

 **9**

D.
11 − 6 =

 **9**

J.
15 − 6 =

 **5**

E.
11 − 2 =

 **3**

K.
5 − 4 =

 **2**

F.
4 − 1 =

 **5**

L.
9 − 4 =

 **1**

Subtracting 1–6

Score

A.
$$10 - 1$$ $$5 - 3$$ $$10 - 4$$ $$13 - 5$$ $$14 - 6$$ $$8 - 5$$

B.
$$6 - 5$$ $$10 - 2$$ $$5 - 2$$ $$9 - 3$$ $$8 - 6$$ $$12 - 4$$

C.
$$9 - 1$$ $$15 - 6$$ $$10 - 5$$ $$6 - 5$$ $$10 - 2$$ $$14 - 5$$

D.
$$8 - 5$$ $$12 - 3$$ $$9 - 5$$ $$8 - 6$$ $$7 - 2$$ $$6 - 6$$

E.
$$4 - 3$$ $$12 - 6$$ $$7 - 6$$ $$8 - 6$$ $$11 - 3$$ $$6 - 5$$

F.
$$2 - 1$$ $$4 - 2$$ $$9 - 5$$ $$13 - 6$$ $$4 - 1$$ $$5 - 3$$

G.
$$10 - 3$$ $$6 - 4$$ $$7 - 5$$ $$10 - 5$$ $$8 - 4$$ $$4 - 2$$

H.
$$6 - 5$$ $$1 - 1$$ $$5 - 4$$ $$8 - 5$$ $$8 - 6$$ $$13 - 6$$

I.
$$12 - 4$$ $$6 - 1$$ $$11 - 5$$ $$3 - 1$$ $$10 - 6$$ $$6 - 5$$

J.
$$7 - 5$$ $$13 - 5$$ $$12 - 6$$ $$4 - 1$$ $$4 - 3$$ $$10 - 5$$

Subtracting 7

A. 10 −7	B. 14 −7	C. 11 −7	D. 16 −7	E. 9 −7
F. 15 −7	G. 8 −7	H. 15 −7	I. 7 −7	J. 8 −7
K. 11 −7	L. 15 −7	M. 9 −7	N. 13 −7	O. 12 −7
P. 16 −7	Q. 14 −7	R. 10 −7	S. 11 −7	T. 7 −7
U. 13 −7	V. 16 −7	W. 8 −7	X. 15 −7	Y. 13 −7

Subtracting 7

Solve each problem.

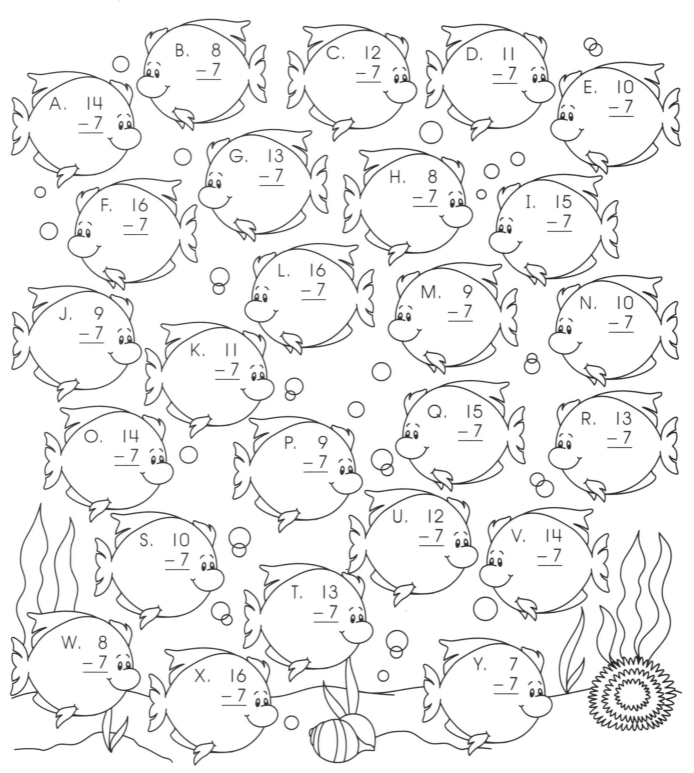

A. 14
− 7

B. 8
− 7

C. 12
− 7

D. 11
− 7

E. 10
− 7

F. 16
− 7

G. 13
− 7

H. 8
− 7

I. 15
− 7

J. 9
− 7

K. 11
− 7

L. 16
− 7

M. 9
− 7

N. 10
− 7

O. 14
− 7

P. 9
− 7

Q. 15
− 7

R. 13
− 7

S. 10
− 7

T. 13
− 7

U. 12
− 7

V. 14
− 7

W. 8
− 7

X. 16
− 7

Y. 7
− 7

Subtracting 7

Solve each problem. Help the children find the zoo.

A.
7 – 7 =

B.
12 – 7 =

C.
13 – 7 =

D.
8 – 7 =

E.
15 – 7 =

J.
11 – 7 =

I.
14 – 7 =

H.
16 – 7 =

G.
9 – 7 =

F.
8 – 7 =

K.
8 – 7 =

L.
15 – 7 =

M.
14 – 7 =

N.
16 – 7 =

O.
10 – 7 =

P.
12 – 7 =

U.
11 – 7 =

T.
8 – 7 =

S.
13 – 7 =

R.
9 – 7 =

Q.
11 – 7 =

V.
12 – 7 =

W.
13 – 7 =

X.
10 – 7 =

Y.
16 – 7 =

1 2 3 4 5 Minutes

Subtracting 7

Score

A.	10 − 7	11 − 7	14 − 7	8 − 7	15 − 7
B.	16 − 7	7 − 7	13 − 7	12 − 7	9 − 7
C.	15 − 7	16 − 7	9 − 7	10 − 7	11 − 7
D.	14 − 7	12 − 7	13 − 7	8 − 7	7 − 7
E.	10 − 7	11 − 7	13 − 7	14 − 7	9 − 7
F.	15 − 7	12 − 7	8 − 7	7 − 7	16 − 7
G.	14 − 7	12 − 7	13 − 7	11 − 7	9 − 7
H.	8 − 7	15 − 7	7 − 7	16 − 7	10 − 7
I.	12 − 7	9 − 7	8 − 7	11 − 7	15 − 7
J.	10 − 7	14 − 7	13 − 7	7 − 7	16 − 7

Name: _____ Date: _____

Subtracting 8

A. 8
   −8

B. 13
   −8

C. 9
   −8

D. 10
   −8

E. 14
   −8

F. 11
   −8

G. 16
   −8

H. 17
   −8

I. 12
   −8

J. 9
   −8

K. 15
   −8

L. 14
   −8

M. 13
   −8

N. 8
   −8

O. 16
   −8

P. 12
   −8

Q. 17
   −8

R. 9
   −8

S. 10
   −8

T. 11
   −8

U. 12
   −8

V. 15
   −8

W. 13
   −8

X. 16
   −8

Y. 10
   −8

Name: _____   Date: _____

Subtracting 8

Solve each problem. Then, color the picture.

A. 9
   − 8

B. 12
   − 8

C. 16
   − 8

D. 14
   − 8

E. 11
   − 8

F. 9
   − 8

G. 12
   − 8

H. 16
   − 8

I. 14
   − 8

J. 11
   − 8

K. 8
   − 8

L. 17
   − 8

M. 10
   − 8

N. 12
   − 8

O. 13
   − 8

P. 11
   − 8

Q. 9
   − 8

R. 17
   − 8

S. 12
   − 8

T. 16
   − 8

U. 14
   − 8

V. 13
   − 8

W. 15
   − 8

X. 17
   − 8

Y. 12
   − 8

Name: _____ Date: _____

Subtracting 8

Solve each problem.

A. 16
  − 8

B. 13
  − 8

C. 17
  − 8

D. 10
  − 8

E. 8
  − 8

F. 14
  − 8

G. 9
  − 8

H. 11
  − 8

I. 15
  − 8

J. 10
  − 8

K. 12
  − 8

L. 15
  − 8

M. 9
  − 8

N. 8
  − 8

O. 16
  − 8

P. 8
  − 8

Q. 14
  − 8

R. 10
  − 8

S. 17
  − 8

T. 11
  − 8

U. 14
  − 8

V. 11
  − 8

W. 13
  − 8

X. 12
  − 8

Y. 16
  − 8

Subtracting 8

Score

A. $16 - 8 =$ $\quad$ $12 - 8 =$ $\quad$ $10 - 8 =$ $\quad$ $14 - 8 =$ $\quad$ $11 - 8 =$

B. $13 - 8 =$ $\quad$ $15 - 8 =$ $\quad$ $9 - 8 =$ $\quad$ $17 - 8 =$ $\quad$ $8 - 8 =$

C. $13 - 8 =$ $\quad$ $14 - 8 =$ $\quad$ $12 - 8 =$ $\quad$ $16 - 8 =$ $\quad$ $11 - 8 =$

D. $15 - 8 =$ $\quad$ $8 - 8 =$ $\quad$ $10 - 8 =$ $\quad$ $9 - 8 =$ $\quad$ $17 - 8 =$

E. $12 - 8 =$ $\quad$ $15 - 8 =$ $\quad$ $8 - 8 =$ $\quad$ $16 - 8 =$ $\quad$ $13 - 8 =$

F. $17 - 8 =$ $\quad$ $14 - 8 =$ $\quad$ $10 - 8 =$ $\quad$ $8 - 8 =$ $\quad$ $11 - 8 =$

G. $13 - 8 =$ $\quad$ $9 - 8 =$ $\quad$ $15 - 8 =$ $\quad$ $8 - 8 =$ $\quad$ $10 - 8 =$

H. $12 - 8 =$ $\quad$ $16 - 8 =$ $\quad$ $11 - 8 =$ $\quad$ $17 - 8 =$ $\quad$ $14 - 8 =$

I. $9 - 8 =$ $\quad$ $8 - 8 =$ $\quad$ $15 - 8 =$ $\quad$ $12 - 8 =$ $\quad$ $14 - 8 =$

J. $16 - 8 =$ $\quad$ $11 - 8 =$ $\quad$ $13 - 8 =$ $\quad$ $10 - 8 =$ $\quad$ $17 - 8 =$

Subtracting 9

Score

A. $\begin{array}{r} 11 \\ -9 \\ \hline \end{array}$ B. $\begin{array}{r} 15 \\ -9 \\ \hline \end{array}$ C. $\begin{array}{r} 12 \\ -9 \\ \hline \end{array}$ D. $\begin{array}{r} 18 \\ -9 \\ \hline \end{array}$ E. $\begin{array}{r} 13 \\ -9 \\ \hline \end{array}$

F. $\begin{array}{r} 14 \\ -9 \\ \hline \end{array}$ G. $\begin{array}{r} 16 \\ -9 \\ \hline \end{array}$ H. $\begin{array}{r} 12 \\ -9 \\ \hline \end{array}$ I. $\begin{array}{r} 11 \\ -9 \\ \hline \end{array}$ J. $\begin{array}{r} 10 \\ -9 \\ \hline \end{array}$

K. $\begin{array}{r} 15 \\ -9 \\ \hline \end{array}$ L. $\begin{array}{r} 13 \\ -9 \\ \hline \end{array}$ M. $\begin{array}{r} 9 \\ -9 \\ \hline \end{array}$ N. $\begin{array}{r} 14 \\ -9 \\ \hline \end{array}$ O. $\begin{array}{r} 17 \\ -9 \\ \hline \end{array}$

P. $\begin{array}{r} 12 \\ -9 \\ \hline \end{array}$ Q. $\begin{array}{r} 16 \\ -9 \\ \hline \end{array}$ R. $\begin{array}{r} 15 \\ -9 \\ \hline \end{array}$ S. $\begin{array}{r} 10 \\ -9 \\ \hline \end{array}$ T. $\begin{array}{r} 9 \\ -9 \\ \hline \end{array}$

U. $\begin{array}{r} 18 \\ -9 \\ \hline \end{array}$ V. $\begin{array}{r} 13 \\ -9 \\ \hline \end{array}$ W. $\begin{array}{r} 11 \\ -9 \\ \hline \end{array}$ X. $\begin{array}{r} 15 \\ -9 \\ \hline \end{array}$ Y. $\begin{array}{r} 16 \\ -9 \\ \hline \end{array}$

Subtracting 9

Solve each problem. Help the bug find the food.

A. 11
   − 9

B. 17
   − 9

C. 13
   − 9

D. 12
   − 9

E. 16
   − 9

F. 14
   − 9

G. 11
   − 9

H. 10
   − 9

I. 15
   − 9

J. 18
   − 9

K. 9
   − 9

L. 10
   − 9

M. 14
   − 9

N. 17
   − 9

O. 12
   − 9

P. 15
   − 9

Q. 13
   − 9

R. 16
   − 9

S. 9
   − 9

T. 18
   − 9

U. 10
   − 9

V. 14
   − 9

W. 17
   − 9

X. 12
   − 9

Y. 9
   − 9

Name: _____ Date: _____

Subtracting 9

Solve each problem. Then, color the picture.

A.
$18 - 9 =$

B. $\begin{array}{r} 11 \\ -\ 9 \\ \hline \end{array}$

C.
$14 - 9 =$

D.
$12 - 9 =$

E. $\begin{array}{r} 16 \\ -\ 9 \\ \hline \end{array}$

F.
$15 - 9 =$

G.
$13 - 9 =$

H.
$10 - 9 =$

I.
$9 - 9 =$

J.
$17 - 9 =$

K.
$12 - 9 =$

L.
$15 - 9 =$

M. $\begin{array}{r} 13 \\ -\ 9 \\ \hline \end{array}$

N.
$16 - 9 =$

O.
$16 - 9 =$

P.
$18 - 9 =$

Q. $\begin{array}{r} 14 \\ -\ 9 \\ \hline \end{array}$

R.
$15 - 9 =$

S.
$10 - 9 =$

T. $\begin{array}{r} 17 \\ -\ 9 \\ \hline \end{array}$

U.
$9 - 9 =$

V.
$11 - 9 =$

W.
$15 - 9 =$

X.
$13 - 9 =$

Subtracting 9

Score

A.
$$9 - 9$$ $$15 - 9$$ $$10 - 9$$ $$13 - 9$$ $$12 - 9$$

B.
$$16 - 9$$ $$18 - 9$$ $$14 - 9$$ $$17 - 9$$ $$11 - 9$$

C.
$$13 - 9$$ $$16 - 9$$ $$9 - 9$$ $$10 - 9$$ $$11 - 9$$

D.
$$12 - 9$$ $$14 - 9$$ $$15 - 9$$ $$18 - 9$$ $$17 - 9$$

E.
$$12 - 9$$ $$11 - 9$$ $$10 - 9$$ $$9 - 9$$ $$17 - 9$$

F.
$$15 - 9$$ $$13 - 9$$ $$18 - 9$$ $$14 - 9$$ $$16 - 9$$

G.
$$12 - 9$$ $$17 - 9$$ $$10 - 9$$ $$9 - 9$$ $$13 - 9$$

H.
$$14 - 9$$ $$15 - 9$$ $$16 - 9$$ $$18 - 9$$ $$11 - 9$$

I.
$$16 - 9$$ $$18 - 9$$ $$13 - 9$$ $$10 - 9$$ $$15 - 9$$

J.
$$9 - 9$$ $$14 - 9$$ $$11 - 9$$ $$12 - 9$$ $$17 - 9$$

Name: _____ Date: _____

Subtracting 7, 8, and 9

1 2 3 4 5
Minutes

A.
$$10 - 7$$
$$15 - 7$$
$$10 - 8$$
$$9 - 7$$
$$13 - 9$$
$$9 - 8$$

B.
$$16 - 7$$
$$14 - 7$$
$$15 - 9$$
$$12 - 7$$
$$18 - 9$$
$$16 - 8$$

C.
$$10 - 9$$
$$15 - 7$$
$$13 - 7$$
$$15 - 8$$
$$14 - 7$$
$$10 - 7$$

D.
$$8 - 7$$
$$17 - 8$$
$$9 - 7$$
$$12 - 9$$
$$10 - 7$$
$$16 - 7$$

E.
$$17 - 9$$
$$15 - 7$$
$$10 - 8$$
$$11 - 9$$
$$9 - 8$$
$$17 - 8$$

F.
$$12 - 9$$
$$15 - 8$$
$$14 - 7$$
$$16 - 9$$
$$8 - 8$$
$$18 - 9$$

G.
$$14 - 8$$
$$13 - 9$$
$$12 - 7$$
$$12 - 9$$
$$8 - 8$$
$$16 - 8$$

H.
$$9 - 7$$
$$10 - 8$$
$$15 - 7$$
$$13 - 7$$
$$14 - 9$$
$$16 - 9$$

I.
$$12 - 8$$
$$10 - 9$$
$$12 - 9$$
$$11 - 8$$
$$10 - 7$$
$$9 - 9$$

J.
$$15 - 8$$
$$18 - 9$$
$$16 - 7$$
$$14 - 7$$
$$13 - 8$$
$$12 - 7$$

Subtracting 7, 8, and 9

Solve each problem. Circle each problem and answer in the puzzle. Problems can be hidden across or down. The first one has been done for you.

A. $16 - 9 = $ **7** $18 - 9 = $ $11 - 9 = $ $15 - 7 = $

B. $12 - 8 = $ $9 - 9 = $ $14 - 7 = $ $16 - 8 = $

C. $15 - 9 = $ $14 - 9 = $ $13 - 8 = $ $15 - 8 = $

Adding and Subtracting 1–9

A.	$9 + 3 =$	$10 - 4 =$	$11 - 6 =$	$7 - 4 =$
B.	$15 - 9 =$	$4 + 4 =$	$13 - 4 =$	$6 + 2 =$
C.	$2 + 4 =$	$8 + 3 =$	$7 - 2 =$	$14 - 5 =$
D.	$12 - 8 =$	$8 - 5 =$	$3 + 7 =$	$15 - 7 =$
E.	$6 - 5 =$	$7 + 4 =$	$3 + 8 =$	$13 - 9 =$
F.	$7 - 7 =$	$6 + 6 =$	$9 + 1 =$	$9 + 6 =$
G.	$16 - 7 =$	$13 - 7 =$	$4 + 6 =$	$8 + 7 =$
H.	$10 - 3 =$	$3 + 6 =$	$9 + 4 =$	$4 - 1 =$
I.	$9 + 5 =$	$3 + 3 =$	$7 - 3 =$	$5 + 6 =$
J.	$5 + 4 =$	$16 - 9 =$	$5 + 2 =$	$3 + 7 =$
K.	$15 - 8 =$	$7 - 2 =$	$11 - 5 =$	$7 + 7 =$
L.	$9 + 2 =$	$9 + 8 =$	$5 + 3 =$	$12 - 7 =$
M.	$3 - 2 =$	$2 + 7 =$	$1 + 1 =$	$4 - 3 =$
N.	$1 + 8 =$	$2 + 1 =$	$2 + 5 =$	$10 - 3 =$
O.	$16 - 8 =$	$4 + 1 =$	$8 + 7 =$	$7 + 7 =$

Page 9

A. 2; B. 6; C. 3; D. 9; E. 4; F. 10; G. 7; H. 3; I. 5; J. 1; K. 6; L. 4; M. 10; N. 5; O. 8; P. 7; Q. 3; R. 2; S. 1; T. 8; U. 9; V. 4; W. 10; X. 6; Y. 3

Page 10

A. 2, 8, 4, 3, 7; B. 5, 10, 1, 6, 9; C. 10, 1, 5, 8, 3; D. 6, 4; E. 7, 2

Page 11

A. 9; B. 5; C. 3; D. 7; E. 2; F. 6; G. 1; H. 4; I. 10; J. 8; K. 3; L. 6; M. 4

Page 12

A. 2, 6, 1, 4, 3; B. 7, 9, 5, 8, 10; C. 4, 7, 10, 1, 2; D. 3, 5, 6, 9, 8; E. 3, 10, 1, 2, 8; F. 6, 4, 9, 5, 7; G. 5, 8, 10, 2, 4; H. 3, 6, 7, 9, 1; I. 7, 8, 4, 1, 6; J. 2, 5, 10, 3, 8

Page 13

A. 2; B. 6; C. 4; D. 8; E. 3; F. 7; G. 5; H. 10; I. 11; J. 9; K. 4; L. 7; M. 9; N. 5; O. 10; P. 8; Q. 6; R. 2; S. 3; T. 11; U. 5; V. 8; W. 10; X. 4; Y. 7

Page 14

A. 6; B. 4; C. 9; D. 3; E. 2; F. 8; G. 5; H. 10; I. 7; J. 11; K. 3; L. 8; M. 4; N. 9; O. 10; P. 6; Q. 11; R. 5; S. 2; T. 6; U. 10; V. 4; W. 5

Page 15

A. 2; B. 9; C. 5; D. 3; E. 10; F. 7; G. 11; H. 4; I. 8; J. 6; K. 4; L. 7; M. 6; N. 8; O. 2; P. 9; Q. 3; R. 11; S. 5; T. 10; U. 3; V. 9; W. 5; X. 4; Y. 8

Page 16

A. 2, 4, 6, 5, 3; B. 8, 10, 7, 9, 11; C. 7, 8, 11, 2, 3; D. 6, 4, 5, 10, 9; E. 4, 11, 5, 6, 9; F. 7, 2, 10, 3, 8; G. 6, 9, 5, 3, 11; H. 4, 7, 10, 8, 2; I. 8, 11, 5, 3, 7; J. 2, 6, 10, 4, 9

Page 17

A. 6; B. 11; C. 8; D. 3; E. 7; F. 4; G. 9; H. 10; I. 5; J. 12; K. 8; L. 7; M. 11; N. 6; O. 9; P. 5; Q. 10; R. 12; S. 3; T. 4; U. 5; V. 8; W. 6; X. 9; Y. 11

Page 18

A. 12; B. 5; C. 9; D. 7; E. 11; F. 4; G. 6; H. 10; I. 3; J. 8; K. 11; L. 4; M. 12; N. 6; O. 10; P. 5; Q. 9; R. 7; S. 3; T. 6

Page 19

A. 7; B. 6; C. 9; D. 12; E. 10; F. 4; G. 3; H. 8; I. 11; J. 5; K. 8; L. 12; M. 5; N. 6; O. 9; P. 11; Q. 7; R. 3; S. 10; T. 4; U. 7; V. 4; W. 11; X. 5; Y. 9

Page 20

A. 9, 5, 3, 7, 4; B. 6, 8, 12, 10, 11; C. 11, 7, 5, 9, 4; D. 8, 6, 3, 12, 10; E. 5, 8, 6, 9, 11; F. 10, 7, 3, 4, 12; G. 4, 12, 8, 6, 11; H. 5, 9, 4, 10, 7; I. 12, 3, 8, 11, 7; J. 9, 4, 10, 3, 5

Page 21

A. 1, 6, 2, 4, 5, 11; B. 7, 5, 8, 10, 11, 8; C. 11, 6, 2, 7, 5, 8; D. 9, 9, 3, 12, 1, 7; E. 10, 6, 3, 11, 11, 7; F. 6, 7, 5, 9, 4, 8; G. 11, 7, 3, 10, 10, 8; H. 4, 2, 6, 3, 7, 9; I. 7, 3, 10, 4, 3, 4; J. 6, 9, 5, 7, 11, 2

Page 22

A. 6, 3, 5, 7, 8; B. 4, 9, 6, 9, 7

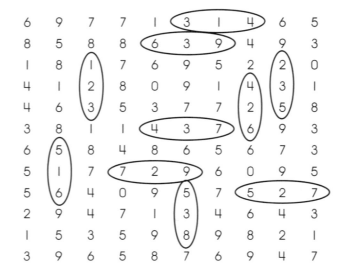

Page 23

A. 7; B. 5; C. 7; D. 7; E. 7; F. 6; G. 6; H. 7; I. 7; J. 7; K. 6; L. 6; M. 6; N. 7; O. 7; P. 5; Q. 5; R. 7; S. 7; T. 7; U. 5; V. 7; W. 7; X. 5; Y. 7; Z. 7

Page 24

A. 4, 7, 1, 9, 9, 8; B. 1, 9, 10, 12, 7, 10; C. 6, 11, 7, 11, 5, 8; D. 4, 2, 7, 9, 1, 6; E. 11, 9, 9, 6, 10, 7; F. 2, 9, 12, 3, 6, 10; G. 6, 6, 1, 2, 9, 8; H. 11, 10, 7, 9, 6, 10; I. 3, 3, 10, 6, 4, 5; J. 4, 7, 11, 5, 10, 7

Page 25

A. 5; B. 6; C. 9; D. 7; E. 12; F. 4; G. 10; H. 5; I. 11; J. 6; K. 13; L. 7; M. 10; N. 5; O. 4; P. 9; Q. 11; R. 8; S. 12; T. 13; U. 10; V. 9; W. 6; X. 4; Y. 7

Page 26

A. 6, 8, 7, 5, 4; B. 12, 13, 7, 10; C. 11, 13, 4; D. 5, 6, 11, 8, 7; E. 10, 13, 5; F. 8, 6, 11, 10, 7

Page 27

A. 11; B. 8; C. 6; D. 10; E. 5; F. 9; G. 7; H. 4; I. 13; J. 11; K. 12; L. 9; M. 7; N. 10; O. 6; P. 11; Q. 4; R. 8; S. 5; T. 13

Page 28

A. 5, 7, 4, 9, 12; B. 5, 6, 11, 4, 8; C. 10, 13, 7, 4, 9; D. 12, 11, 13, 8, 5; E. 6, 10, 11, 13, 7; F. 8, 12, 10, 5, 4; G. 6, 11, 13, 12, 4; H. 9, 8, 10, 9, 7; I. 8, 11, 7, 5, 6; J. 9, 5, 12, 13, 4

Page 29

A. 5; B. 6; C. 7; D. 13; E. 11; F. 14; G. 10; H. 9; I. 8; J. 5; K. 7; L. 5; M. 14; N. 9; O. 12; P. 7; Q. 6; R. 10; S. 13; T. 11; U. 12; V. 13; W. 9; X. 12; Y. 6

Page 30

A. 9; B. 7; C. 11; D. 9; E. 14; F. 5; G. 6; H. 13; I. 14; J. 5; K. 9; L. 12; M. 7; N. 8; O. 11; P. 13; Q. 5; R. 9; S. 12; T. 7; U. 14; V. 6

Page 31

A. 13, 9, 7, 11, 10; B. 10, 8, 5, 14, 12; C. 7, 10, 8; D. 11, 13, 12; E. 13, 8, 7; F. 9, 5, 11; G. 14, 10, 8

Page 32

A. 9, 10, 5, 8, 7; B. 11, 13, 9, 12, 14; C. 8, 11, 14, 5, 10; D. 7, 9, 10, 13, 12; E. 7, 14, 5, 10, 12; F. 10, 8, 13, 9, 11; G. 9, 12, 14, 10, 8; H. 7, 6, 11, 13, 5; I. 11, 2, 8, 5, 10; J. 5, 9, 14, 7, 12

Page 33

A. 6; B. 10; C. 8; D. 12; E. 7; F. 11; G. 9; H. 14; I. 15; J. 13; K. 12; L. 11; M. 13; N. 9; O. 14; P. 8; Q. 10; R. 6; S. 7; T. 15; U. 9; V. 8; W. 14; X. 12; Y. 11

Page 34

A. 10; B. 12; C. 13; D. 7; E. 12; F. 6; G. 9; H. 14; I. 11; J. 15; K. 7; L. 12; M. 10; N. 13; O. 14; P. 10; Q. 15; R. 11; S. 6; T. 9

Page 35

A. 6; B. 13; C. 7; D. 14; E. 11; F. 9; G. 12; H. 9; I. 11; J. 15; K. 10; L. 10; M. 6; N. 12; O. 13; P. 1; Q. 12; R. 9; S. 13; T. 15; U. 9; V. 14; W. 7

Page 36

A. 6, 8, 10, 9, 7; B. 12, 14, 11, 13, 15; C. 11, 12, 15, 6, 7; D. 10, 8, 9, 14, 13; E. 12, 15, 9, 10, 13; F. 11, 6, 14, 7, 8; G. 10, 13, 8, 7, 15; H. 12, 11, 15, 13, 6; I. 14, 15, 9, 7, 11; J. 6, 10, 12, 8, 13

Page 37

A. 5, 8, 4, 11, 10, 13; B. 14, 10, 14, 10, 7, 6; C. 9, 11, 13, 7, 9, 15; D. 5, 11, 13, 6, 6, 14; E. 5, 11, 8, 7, 11, 12; F. 11, 14, 5, 10, 9, 5; G. 12, 10, 11, 4, 10, 9; H. 9, 9, 9, 5, 14, 8; I. 6, 13, 9, 8, 10, 5; J. 13, 7, 11, 8, 7, 14

Page 38

A. 6, 9, 6, 8, 7; B. 12, 5, 8, 6, 9

6	4	5	①	5	6	10	2	6	2
6	5	8	8	3	3	⓪	4	9	3
11	8	②	4	6	7	6	4	6	10
4	11	12	1	7	9	6	5	②	5
4	6	2	3	2	③	6	9	6	8
7	3	6	10	4	2	1	5	8	3
3	6	6	5	8	⑤	4	9	7	3
3	①	6	7	2	2	6	1	11	④
8	6	3	1	5	①	11	6	8	4
2	5	6	4	9	4	8	6	4	8
7	5	3	2	9	5	3	10	12	11
4	7	2	4	2	1	4	9	3	1

Page 39

A. 9; B. 9; C. 8; D. 9; E. 9; F. 8; G. 8; H. 8; I. 8; J. 8; K. 8; L. 8; M. 8; N. 9; O. 8; P. 8; Q. 8; R. 9; S. 8; T. 8; U. 9; V. 9; W. 7; X. 7; Y. 7; Z. 7

Page 40

A. 7, 7, 7, 6, 6, 8; B. 5, 10, 11, 15, 7, 13; C. 9, 12, 7, 13, 8, 11; D. 8, 5, 7, 7, 5, 7; E. 14, 12, 9, 8, 12, 8; F. 5, 11, 10, 8, 6, 11; G. 6, 7, 5, 10, 11, 10; H. 8, 7, 7, 7, 6, 12; I. 6, 11, 14, 6, 8, 9; J. 6, 7, 10, 7, 8, 10

Page 41

A. 11; B. 3; C. 12; D. 6; E. 4; F. 5; G. 4; H. 9; I. 10; J. 13; K. 2; L. 14

Page 42

A. 1, 8, 4, 8, 10, 9; B. 11, 2, 7, 12, 14, 6; C. 10, 10, 7, 10, 2, 11; D. 13, 6, 9, 15, 2, 11; E. 4, 4, 3, 14, 4, 11; F. 2, 5, 14, 6, 5, 14; G. 4, 10, 9, 5, 12, 6; H. 11, 4, 10, 13, 6, 6; I. 6, 6, 6, 6, 6, 11; J. 9, 8, 8, 5, 7, 9

Page 43

A. 7; B. 11; C. 14; D. 13; E. 8; F. 12; G. 10; H. 15; I. 16; J. 14; K. 8; L. 12; M. 14; N. 10; O. 15; P. 13; Q. 11; R. 7; S. 8; T. 16; U. 10; V. 13; W. 15; X. 14; Y. 12

Answer Key

Page 44

A. 11, 14, 9, 8, 7; B. 13, 10, 15, 12, 16; C. 8, 13, 14, 7, 11; D. 16, 10, 12; E. 7, 15, 9; F. 11, 7, 14; G. 16, 9, 11; H. 13, 8, 10

Page 45

A. 7; B. 9; C. 10; D. 15; E. 12; F. 16; G. 14; H. 13; I. 11; J. 8; K. 14; L. 12; M. 11; N. 13; O. 7; P. 9; Q. 8; R. 16; S. 10; T. 15; U. 8; V. 14; W. 10; X. 11

Page 46

A. 7, 9, 11, 10, 8, 13; B. 15, 12, 9, 16, 12, 14; C. 16, 7, 8, 11, 9, 10; D. 15, 14, 13, 12, 13, 11; E. 8, 12, 7, 15, 8, 13; F. 11, 9, 10, 14, 16, 11; G. 13, 15, 13, 7, 14, 16; H. 10, 8, 12, 9, 11, 15; I. 7, 9, 13, 15, 8, 16; J. 9, 11, 10, 12, 14, 15

Page 47

A. 16; B. 11; C. 13; D. 8; E. 12; F. 9; G. 14; H. 15; I. 10; J. 17; K. 13; L. 12; M. 11; N. 16; O. 14; P. 10; Q. 15; R. 17; S. 8; T. 9; U. 10; V. 13; W. 11; X. 14; Y. 8

Page 48

A. 9; B. 13; C. 9; D. 11; E. 10; F. 14; G. 8; H. 14; I. 11; J. 15; K. 11; L. 16; M. 10; N. 14; O. 13; P. 16; Q. 17; R. 12

Page 49

A. 14; B. 11; C. 15; D. 8; E. 16; F. 12; G. 17; H. 9; I. 13; J. 10; K. 11; L. 13; M. 17; N. 16; O. 14; P. 16; Q. 12; R. 8; S. 15; T. 9; U. 12; V. 9; W. 11; X. 10; Y. 14

Page 50

A. 14, 10, 8, 12, 9; B. 11, 13, 17, 15, 16; C. 11, 12, 10, 14, 17; D. 13, 16, 8, 17, 15; E. 10, 13, 16, 11, 9; F. 15, 14, 8, 12, 14; G. 9, 17, 13, 16, 8; H. 10, 14, 9, 15, 12; I. 17, 8, 13, 15, 12; J. 14, 9, 11, 8, 10

Page 51

A. 10; B. 14; C. 11; D. 17; E. 12; F. 10; G. 15; H. 11; I. 13; J. 9; K. 14; L. 12; M. 18; N. 13; O. 16; P. 11; Q. 15; R. 12; S. 9; T. 16; U. 17; V. 12; W. 18; X. 14; Y. 11

Page 52

A. 10; B. 16; C. 12; D. 11; E. 15; F. 13; G. 10; H. 9; I. 14; J. 17; K. 18; L. 9; M. 13; N. 16; O. 11; P. 14; Q. 12; R. 15; S. 18; T. 17; U. 9; V. 13; W. 16; X. 11; Y. 18

Page 53

A. 17; B. 13; C. 11; D. 15; E. 14; F. 10; G. 9; H. 18; I. 14; J. 12; K. 16; L. 11; M. 15; N. 13; O. 12; P. 17; Q. 9; R. 18; S. 14; T. 12; U. 11; V. 10; W. 17; X. 15

Page 54

A. 18, 14, 9, 12, 11; B. 15, 17, 13, 16, 10; C. 12, 15, 18, 9, 10; D. 11, 13, 14, 17, 16; E. 11, 10, 9, 18, 16; F. 14, 12, 17, 13, 15; G. 11, 16, 9, 18, 12; H. 13, 14, 15, 17, 9; I. 15, 16, 12, 9, 14; J. 18, 13, 10, 11, 17

Page 55

A. 7, 12, 8, 16, 12, 17; B. 13, 11, 14, 9, 17, 14; C. 9, 12, 10, 13, 11, 11; D. 15, 15, 14, 11, 18, 13; E. 16, 12, 8, 10, 17, 13; F. 11, 13, 11, 15, 16, 14; G. 12, 12, 9, 11, 16, 14; H. 16, 8, 12, 10, 13, 15; I. 10, 9, 11, 9, 7, 11; J. 13, 17, 15, 11, 11, 8

Page 56

A. 15, 17, 15, 13, 10; B. 13, 16, 10, 14, 14

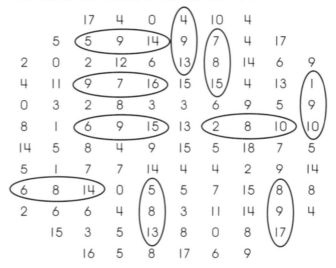

Page 57

A. 16; B. 16; C. 16; D. 10; E. 10; F. 10; G. 16; H. 10; I. 16; J. 10; K. 16; L. 12; M. 16; N. 16; O. 16; P. 16; Q. 16; R. 15; S. 16; T. 15; U. 16; V. 16; W. 12; X. 12; Y. 15; Z. 15

Page 58

A. 16, 11, 7, 15, 15, 14; B. 9, 15, 14, 10, 13, 10; C. 12, 18, 13, 17, 11, 14; D. 16, 8, 13, 15, 7, 12; E. 17, 15, 15, 12, 11, 13; F. 14, 11, 11, 15, 12, 16; G. 12, 10, 7, 8, 15, 14; H. 17, 16, 13, 15, 12, 8; I. 15, 9, 16, 9, 14, 17; J. 16, 13, 17, 11, 12, 9

Page 59

A. 11, 9, 15, 6, 11; B. 5, 9, 9, 12, 4; C. 9, 10, 13, 2, 14; D. 12, 11, 5, 10, 7; E. 12, 12, 15, 7, 13; F. 5, 13, 9, 14, 16; Car F wins.

Answer Key

Page 60
A. 1, 8, 9, 8, 10, 9; B. 11, 8, 7, 12, 14, 6; C. 10, 12, 7, 10, 11, 5; D. 13, 10, 9, 15, 10, 11; E. 4, 10, 3, 14, 12, 13; F. 2, 5, 14, 6, 5, 14; G. 4, 10, 9, 9, 12, 11; H. 11, 4, 10, 13, 6, 14; I. 6, 9, 6, 6, 7, 11; J. 9, 18, 8, 5, 7, 12

Page 61
A. 9; B. 4; C. 1; D. 7; E. 2; F. 8; G. 5; H. 1; I. 3; J. 5; K. 4; L. 2; M. 8; N. 7; O. 6; P. 1; Q. 5; R. 0; S. 3; T. 8; U. 7; V. 2; W. 8; X. 4; Y. 1

Page 62
A. 0, 6, 2, 1, 5; B. 3, 8, 3, 4, 7; C. 8, 5, 3, 6. 1; D. 4, 2, 5, 9; E. 7, 1, 3; F. 6, 1, 8

Page 63
A. 7; B. 3; C. 1; D. 5; E. 9; F. 4; G. 2; H. 5; I. 8; J. 6; K. 1; L. 4; M. 2; N. 5; O. 7; P. 6; Q. 3; R. 9; S. 0; T. 8

Page 64
A. 0, 4, 5, 2, 1; B. 5, 7, 3, 6, 8; C. 2, 5, 8, 6, 0; D. 1, 3, 4, 7, 6; E. 1, 8, 3, 0, 6; F. 4, 2, 7, 3, 5; G. 3, 6, 8, 1, 2; H. 1, 4, 5, 7, 0; I. 5, 6, 2, 3, 4; J. 0, 3, 8, 1. 7

Page 65
A. 1; B. 2; C. 0; D. 4; E. 6; F. 3; G. 1; H. 6; I. 7; J. 5; K. 9; L. 3; M. 5; N. 1; O. 6; P. 4; Q. 2; R. 7; S. 2; T. 8; U. 1; V. 4; W. 6; X. 0; Y. 3

Page 66
A. 2; B. 5; C. 3; D. 7; E. 4; F. 9; G. 1; H. 3; I. 6; J. 2; K. 6; L. 7; M. 4; N. 0; O. 5; P. 2; Q. 7; R. 3; S. 8; T. 6; U. 7; V. 2; W. 6; X. 0; Y. 9

Page 67
A. 2; B. 5; C. 1; D. 8; E. 3; F. 7; G. 0; H. 2; I. 0; J. 3; K. 5; L. 0; M. 3; N. 2; O. 4; P. 6; Q. 5; R. 9; S. 8; T. 3; U. 7; V. 1; W. 3; X. 5; Y. 4

Page 68
A. 5, 0, 2, 1, 9; B. 4, 6, 3, 8, 7; C. 3, 8, 7, 9, 4; D. 2, 0, 1, 6, 5; E. 0, 7, 1, 2, 5; F. 3, 6, 9, 7, 4; G. 2. 5, 1, 4, 8; H. 0, 3, 6, 7, 9; I. 2, 9, 1, 4, 8; J. 7, 3, 6, 0, 5

Page 69
A. 0; B. 5; C. 2; D. 6; E. 1; F. 3; G. 6; H. 4. I. 0; J. 8; K. 2; L. 1; M. 5; N. 0; O. 3; P. 1; Q. 9; R. 6; S. 5; T. 4; U. 3; V. 2; W. 7; X. 3; Y. 5

Page 70
A. 6; B. 8; C. 3; D. 1; E. 5; F. 1; G. 0; H. 4; I. 6; J. 7; K. 2; L. 5; M. 4; N. 6; O. 8; P. 4; Q. 6; R. 9; S. 4; T. 2

Page 71
A. 3; B. 7; C. 4; D. 1; E. 8; F. 9; G. 2; H. 6; I. 3; J. 7; K. 4; L. 2; M. 6; N. 0; O. 3; P. 5; Q. 4; R. 2; S. 1; T. 6; U. 1; V. 3; W. 5; X. 4; Y. 9

Page 72
A. 3, 7, 6, 1, 8; B. 0, 2, 9, 4, 5; C. 2, 1, 3, 8, 9; D. 6, 0, 5, 7, 4; E. 3, 2, 9, 7, 5; F. 4, 1, 6, 1, 8; G. 7, 6, 2, 9, 8; H. 3, 5, 0, 4, 1; I. 6, 5, 2, 9, 1; J. 0, 7, 4, 8, 3

Page 73
A. 9, 4, 7, 2, 2, 7; B. 5, 8, 2, 8, 5, 4; C. 8, 4, 0, 3, 3, 2; D. 7, 9, 1, 6, 8, 5; E. 4, 4, 1, 5, 7, 7; F. 0, 8, 3, 3, 0, 5; G. 7, 1, 1, 6, 6, 8; H. 2, 7, 4, 1, 9, 3; I. 3, 2, 8, 0, 8, 8; J. 8, 7, 3, 1, 9, 6

Page 74
A. 1, 1, 2, 5, 0; B. 5, 3, 2, 4, 7

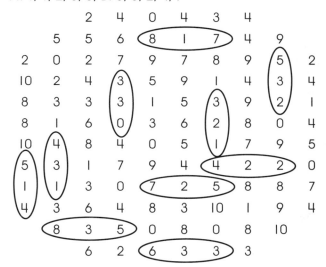

Page 75
A. 6; B. 6; C. 4; D. 4; E. 6; F. 6; G. 6; H. 6; I. 4; J. 4; K. 4; L. 4; M. 6; N. 4; O. 4; P. 4; Q. 4; R. 6; S. 6; T. 4; U. 6; V. 2; W. 2; X. 2; Y. 2; Z. 2

Page 76
A. 2, 3, 9, 7, 8, 4; B. 8, 3, 5, 6, 1, 9; C. 4, 5, 5, 7, 3, 2; D. 0, 8, 1, 5, 7, 8; E. 7, 7, 3, 2, 6, 5; F. 9, 5, 6, 1, 2, 4; G. 4, 9, 9, 9, 3, 6; H. 5, 3, 0, 7, 2, 8; I. 9, 1, 8, 4, 2, 1; J. 0, 5, 5, 9, 4, 1

Page 77
A. 3; B. 8; C. 1; D. 2; E. 4; F. 6; G. 2; H. 7; I. 3; J. 0; K. 5; L. 9; M. 2; N. 5; O. 6; P. 1; Q. 9; R. 0; S. 4; T. 5; U. 2; V. 1; W. 7; X. 6; Y. 0

Page 78

A. 8; B. 0; C. 9; D. 5; E. 6; F. 4; G. 5; H. I; I. 2; J. 3;
K. 5; L. 6; M. 7; N. 0; O. 3; P. 5; Q. 9; R. 2; S. 5; T. 7;
U. 0; V. 8; W. 3; X. 2; Y. 9

Page 79

A. 3; B. 0; C. 8; D. 2; E. 7; F. I; G. 9; H. 6; I. 5; J. 3;
K. 4; L. I; M. 9; N. 2; 0. 8; P. 3; Q. 0; R. 6; S. 7; T. 5

Page 80

A. 4, 8, 5, I, 2; B. 7, 6, 3, 9, 0; C. 2, 5, 9, 6, I; D. 4, 3,
6, 0, 7; E. 8, 2, 3, 6, 5; F. 0, 4, I, 7, 9; G. 9, 3, 5, 4, 8;
H. 2, 0, 7, I, 6; I. 0, 3, 9, 7, 8; J. I, 6, 4, 5, 2

Page 81

A. 5; B. 4; C. 7; D. 3; E. I; F. 4; G. 0; H. 9; I. 8; J. 5;
K. 7; L. 5; M. 4; N. 9; O. 2; P. 0; Q. 5; R. 0; S. 3; T. I;
U. 2; V. 3; W. 9; X. 2; Y. 6

Page 82

A. 6; B. 2; C. 8; D. 7; E. I; F. 9; G. 4; H. 5; I. 4; J. 5;
K. 9; L. 6; M. 3; N. 0; O. 2; P. 7; Q. 9; R. 6; S. 3; T. 5;
U. 8; V. I; W. 2; X. 7; Y. 4

Page 83

A. 3, 9, 7, I; B. 0, 2, 8, 5; C. 4, 2, 7, 0; D. 8, I, 3, 2;
E. 9, 5, 0; F. 4, 0; G. 8, 3; H. 7, I

Page 84

A. 4, 0, 5, 8, 7; B. I, 3, 9, 2, 6; C. 8, I, 4, 5, 0; D. 2, 9,
6, 3, 7; E. 7, 4, 5, 0, 2; F. 6, 8, 3, 9, I; G. 9, 2, 4, 6, 8;
H. 7, 0, I, 3, 5; I. I, 6, 8, 5, 0; J. 3, 9, 4, 7, 2

Page 85

A. 4; B. 8; C. 6; D. 0; E. 5; F. 9; G. 7; H. 2; I. 3; J. I;
K. 0; L. 9; M. I; N. 7; O. 2; P. 6; Q. 8; R. 4; S. 5; T. 3;
U. 7; V. 6; W. 2; X. 0; Y. 9

Page 86

A. 8; B. 0; C. I; D. 5; E. 4; F. 0; G. 7; H. 2; I. 9; J. 3;
K. 5; L. 0; M. 3; N. I; O. 2; P. 8; Q. 3; R. 9; S. 4; T. 7;
U. 4; V. 8; W. 2; X. 0; Y. 3

Page 87

A. I; B. 2; C. 4; D. 7; E. 9; F. 3; G. 8; H. 5; I. 0; J. 3;
K. 8; L. 5; M. 9; N. 8; O. 4; P. I; Q. 0; R. 3; S. 7; T. 5;
U. 7; V. 0; W. 9; X. 5; Y. I

Page 88

A. 4, I, 8, 7, 5; B. 0, 2, 9, 6, 3; C. 9, 0, 3, 4, 5; D. 8, 6,
7, 2, I; E. 0, 3, 7, 8, I; F. 9, 4, 2, 5, 6; G. 8, I, 7, 0, 3;
H. 5, 9, 2, 6, 4; I. 0, 3, 7, 5, 9; J. 4, 8, 2, 0, 6

Page 89

A. 5, 8, 6, I, 8, 5; B. I, 0, 7, 4, 2, 2; C. 4, 2, 7, 7, 2, 9;
D. 3, 9, 9, 3, 5, I; E. I, 0, 4, 2, 7, I; F. 6, 5, 9, 0, 3, 2;
G. 7, 2, 9, 5, 4, 2; H. I, 6, I, 9, I, 4; I. I, 9, 9, 7, 4, I;
J. 9, 8, 2, 3, 4, 4

Page 90

A. 2, 6, 3, 7; B. 8, 7, 2, 5; C. 4, 7, 4, 4

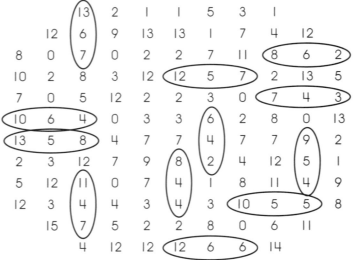

Page 91

A. 3; B. 3; C. 3; D. 4; E. 2; F. 3; G. I; H. 4; I. 4; J. I;
K. 3; L. 3; M. I; N. I; O. I; P. 3; Q. 2; R. I; S. I; T. 2;
U. 3; V. 2; W. 2; X. 4; Y. 4; Z. 4

Page 92

A. 9, 7, 2, I, 8, 3; B. 5, 2, 0, 3, 9, 6; C. I, 4, 5, 5, 3, 2;
D. 6, 5, 4, 7, 2, 2; E. 4, I, 7, I, 4, 6; F. 6, 3, I, 6, 7, 3;
G. 6, 9, I, 3, I, 3; H. 6, 4, 2, 3, 7, I; I. 8, I, 4, 6, 9, 7;
J. 8, 2, 2, 9, 2, 2

Page 93

A. I; B. 7; C. 0; D. 5; E. 9; F. 3; G. 6; H. 8; I. 2; J. 9;
K. I; L. 5

Page 94

A. 9, 2, 6, 8, 8, 3; B. I, 8, 3, 6, 2, 8; C. 8, 9, 5, I, 8, 9;
D. 3, 9, 4, 2, 5, 0; E. I, 6, I, 2, 8, I; F. I, 2, 4, 7, 3, 2;
G. 7, 2, 2, 5, 4, 2; H. I, 0, I, 3, 2, 7; I. 8, 5, 6, 2, 4, I;
J. 2, 8, 6, 3, I, 5

Page 95

A. 3; B. 7; C. 4; D. 9; E. 2; F. 8; G. I; H. 8; I. 0; J. I;
K. 4; L. 8; M. 2; N. 6; O. 5; P. 9; Q. 7; R. 3; S. 4; T. 0;
U. 6; V. 9; W. I; X. 8; Y. 6

Answer Key

Page 96

A. 7; B. 1; C. 5; D. 4; E. 3; F. 9; G. 6; H. 1; I. 8; J. 2;
K. 4; L. 9; M. 2; N. 3; O. 7; P. 2; Q. 8; R. 6; S. 3; T. 6;
U. 5; V. 7; W. 1; X. 9; Y. 0

Page 97

A. 0; B. 5; C. 6; D. 1; E. 8; F. 1; G. 2; H. 9; I. 7; J. 4;
K. 1; L. 8; M. 7; N. 9; O. 3; P. 5; Q. 4; R. 2; S. 6; T. 1;
U. 4; V. 5; W. 6; X. 3; Y. 9

Page 98

A. 3, 4, 7, 1, 8; B. 9, 0, 6, 5, 2; C. 8, 9, 2, 3, 4; D. 7, 5,
6, 1, 0; E. 3, 4, 6, 7, 2; F. 8, 5, 1, 0, 9; G. 7, 5, 6, 4, 2;
H. 1, 8, 0, 9, 3; I. 5, 2, 1, 4, 8; J. 3, 7, 6, 0, 9

Page 99

A. 0; B. 5; C. 1; D. 2; E. 6; F. 3; G. 8; H. 9; I. 4; J. 1;
K. 7; L. 6; M. 5; N. 0; O. 8; P. 4; Q. 9; R. 1; S. 2; T. 3;
U. 4; V. 7; W. 5; X. 8; Y. 2

Page 100

A. 1; B. 4; C. 8; D. 6; E. 3; F. 1; G. 4; H. 8; I. 6; J. 3;
K. 0; L. 9; M. 2; N. 4; O. 5; P. 3; Q. 1; R. 9; S. 4; T. 8;
U. 6; V. 5; W. 7; X. 9; Y. 4

Page 101

A. 8; B. 5; C. 9; D. 2; E. 0; F. 6; G. 1; H. 3; I. 7; J. 2;
K. 4; L. 7; M. 1; N. 0; O. 8; P. 0; Q. 6; R. 2; S. 9; T. 3;
U. 6; V. 3; W. 5; X. 4; Y. 8

Page 102

A. 8, 4, 2, 6, 3; B. 5, 7, 1, 9, 0; C. 5, 6, 4, 8, 3; D. 7, 0,
2, 1, 9; E. 4, 7, 0, 8, 5; F. 9, 6, 2, 0, 3; G. 5, 1, 7, 0, 2;
H. 4, 8, 3, 9, 6; I. 1, 0, 7, 4, 6; J. 8, 3, 5, 2, 9

Page 103

A. 2; B. 6; C. 3; D. 9; E. 4; F. 5; G. 7; H. 3; I. 2; J. 1;
K. 6; L. 4; M. 0; N. 5; O. 8; P. 3; Q. 7; R. 6; S. 1; T. 0;
U. 9; V. 4; W. 2; X. 6; Y. 7

Page 104

A. 2; B. 8; C. 4; D. 3; E. 7; F. 5; G. 2; H. 1; I. 6; J. 9;
K. 0; L. 1; M. 5; N. 8; O. 3; P. 6; Q. 4; R. 7; S. 0; T. 9;
U. 1; V. 5; W. 8; X. 3; Y. 0

Page 105

A. 9; B. 2; C. 5; D. 3; E. 7; F. 6; G. 4; H. 1; I. 0; J. 8;
K. 3; L. 6; M. 4; N. 7; O. 7; P. 9; Q. 5; R. 6; S. 1; T. 8;
U. 0; V. 2; W. 6; X. 4

Page 106

A. 0, 6, 1, 4, 3; B. 7, 9, 5, 8, 2; C. 4, 7, 0, 1, 2; D. 3, 5,
6, 9, 8; E. 3, 2, 1, 0, 8; F. 6, 4, 9, 5, 7; G. 3, 8, 1, 0, 4;
H. 5, 6, 7, 9, 2; I. 7, 9, 4, 1, 6; J. 0, 5, 2, 3, 8

Page 107

A. 3, 8, 2, 2, 4, 1; B. 9, 7, 6, 5, 9, 8; C. 1, 8, 6, 7, 7, 3;
D. 1, 9, 2, 3, 3, 9; E. 8, 8, 2, 2, 1, 9; F. 3, 7, 7, 7, 0, 9;
G. 6, 4, 5, 3, 0, 8; H. 2, 2, 8, 6, 5, 7; I. 4, 1, 3, 3, 3, 0;
J. 7, 9, 9, 7, 5, 5

Page 108

A. 7, 9, 2, 8; B. 4, 0, 7, 8; C. 6, 5, 5, 7

6	9	7	4	12	3	10	4	5	5
16	9	7	8	6	3	11	9	2	10
9	8	1	7	13	7	17	2	2	0
4	1	15	5	8	9	16	14	3	1
8	3	9	18	5	17	7	9	5	8
14	8	6	1	4	3	9	16	11	3
9	5	8	4	9	9	0	8	7	3
5	15	7	8	2	9	6	8	12	14
5	6	3	0	15	8	7	5	12	7
2	13	4	16	1	3	4	6	7	7
1	9	3	5	18	9	9	16	5	1
13	5	12	5	9	13	6	12	8	4

Page 109

A. 4; B. 4; C. 4; D. 4; E. 3; F. 3; G. 4; H. 2; I. 2; J. 4;
K. 2; L. 2; M. 2; N. 4; O. 2; P. 2; Q. 2; R. 4; S. 4; T. 2;
U. 2; V. 2; W. 4; X. 2; Y. 2; Z. 4

Page 110

A. 2, 5, 3, 1, 9, 8; B. 3, 7, 0, 2, 5, 4; C. 8, 9, 9, 1, 7, 6;
D. 0, 2, 5, 9, 3, 4; E. 1, 1, 7, 6, 5, 8; F. 0, 5, 3, 1, 6, 8;
G. 8, 2, 3, 2, 7, 0; H. 9, 8, 7, 1, 6, 4; I. 1, 1, 2, 5, 2, 1;
J. 0, 9, 9, 7, 4, 5

Page 111

A. 1, 1, 8, 4, 5, 3; B. 7, 3, 8, 0, 8, 0; C. 5, 0, 4, 0, 1, 9;
D. 4, 7, 6, 6, 1, 5; E. 7, 3, 0, 7, 1, 2; F. 4, 8, 8, 5, 0, 1;
Horse C wins.

Page 112

A. 9, 2, 1, 8, 8, 9; B. 1, 2, 3, 6, 2, 8; C. 8, 8, 7, 0, 7, 9;
D. 3, 4, 9, 3, 6, 1; E. 8, 4, 7, 2, 8, 9; F. 8, 3, 4, 0, 3, 2;
G. 8, 2, 9, 3, 4, 3; H. 1, 6, 0, 3, 2, 8; I. 8, 3, 6, 2, 3, 1;
J. 9, 0, 6, 3, 1, 3

Page 113

A. 4, 12, 2, 16, 4; B. 11, 9, 11, 6, 9; C. 5, 14, 6, 8, 5;
D. 7, 2, 3, 1, 15; E. 6, 3, 3, 4, 8; F. 2, 0, 2, 15, 1; G. 3,
6, 14, 7, 16; H. 9, 6, 7, 5, 7; I. 0, 14, 2, 5, 1; J. 14, 5, 4,
13, 6

Page 114

A. 7, 8, 4, 2, 12; B. 13, 3, 7, 6, 10; C. 4, 7, 6, 1, 9; D. 3,
4, 4, 15, 8; E. 12, 3, 5, 14, 5; F. 13, 14, 1, 8, 7; G. 9, 9, 6,
0, 13; H. 10, 8, 8, 3, 7; I. 1, 8, 9, 6, 3; J. 9, 4, 10, 4, 11

Page 115

A. 5, 11, 8, 16, 2; B. 11, 5, 9, 7, 5; C. 4, 17, 12, 5, 14;
D. 2, 2, 9, 8, 8; E. 3, 18, 10, 9, 8; F. 14, 7, 0, 13, 5;
G. 8, 9, 6, 4, 13; H. 5, 6, 12, 2, 6; I. 2, 10, 17, 15, 9;
J. 16, 2, 4, 3, 10

Page 116

A. 15, 8, 10, 9, 3; B. 6, 7, 8, 10, 10; C. 4, 0, 12, 12, 9;
D. 9, 5, 9, 13, 9; E. 11, 2, 7, 4, 8; F. 7, 13, 9, 3, 7; G. 5,
10, 8, 8, 0; H. 6, 1, 7, 4, 7; I. 2, 10, 8, 7, 5; J. 10, 8, 11,
4, 3

Page 117

A. 8, 6, 7, 11, 5; B. 6, 12, 11, 7, 4; C. 12, 3, 7, 9, 7; D. 2,
5, 4, 10, 9; E. 12, 8, 9, 5, 5; F. 10, 17, 4, 5, 5; G. 7, 5, 6,
13, 9; H. 0, 14, 7, 3, 6; I. 7, 15, 9, 16, 3; J. 8, 8, 5, 9, 14

Page 118

A. 12, 7, 7, 9; B. 2, 7, 8, 6; C. 11, 8, 16, 7; D. 6, 7, 4, 8;
E. 6, 7, 17, 9; F. 9, 1, 16, 2; G. 9, 15, 1, 4; H. 2, 6, 2, 9;
I. 7, 6, 1, 12; J. 7, 11, 3, 9; K. 8, 8, 6, 12; L. 5, 6, 5, 8;
M. 5, 17, 7, 4; N. 8, 2, 6, 4; O. 6, 9, 11, 3

Page 119

A. 10, 7, 6, 9, 7, 7; B. 6, 12, 6, 17, 9, 6; C. 9, 3, 8, 4, 7,
5; D. 16, 6, 9, 5, 9, 3; E. 3, 9, 11, 9, 8, 10; F. 6, 3, 7, 11,
7, 13; G. 13, 12, 1, 6, 9, 4; H. 5, 11, 7, 12, 6, 8; I. 9, 11,
15, 9, 10, 2; J. 5, 12, 5, 10, 3, 7

Page 120

A. 4, 4, 8, 9, 8, 9; B. 6, 2, 8, 10, 13, 9; C. 17, 5, 10, 7, 7,
1; D. 10, 7, 18, 7, 2, 14; E. 5, 7, 6, 12, 2, 5; F. 14, 4, 9, 9,
5, 10; G. 8, 9, 0, 11, 10, 4; H. 4, 10, 13, 9, 9, 11; I. 8, 12,
8, 7, 4, 1; J. 11, 6, 8, 9, 15, 0

Page 121

A. 12, 6, 5, 3; B. 6, 8, 9, 8; C. 6, 11, 5, 9; D. 4, 3, 10, 8;
E. 1, 11, 11, 4; F. 0, 12, 10, 15; G. 9, 6, 10, 15; H. 7, 9,
13, 3; I. 14, 6, 4, 11; J. 9, 7, 7, 10; K. 7, 5, 6, 14; L. 11,
17, 8, 5; M. 1, 9, 2, 1; N. 9, 3, 7, 7; O. 8, 5, 15, 14